THE CENTRAL INTELLIGENCE AGENCY

A Photographic History

THE
CENTRAL
INTELLIGENCE
AGENCY

A Photographic History

JOHN PATRICK QUIRK

DAVID ATLEE PHILLIPS   DR. RAY CLINE

WALTER PFORZHEIMER

Published by

Foreign Intelligence Press
The Puritan Lodge
42 Boston Post Rd.
Guilford, Connecticut 06437

United States of America

ISBN 0-89568-500-0

Printed in Yugoslavia by: BIGZ — Grafoimpex
Production: Arelis Spencer

Library of Congress Cataloging-in-Publication Data

The Central Intelligence Agency.
   Includes index.
   1. United States. Central Intelligence Agency History. I.

JK468. I6C455 1986   327.1'2'06073   86-4697   ISBN
0-89568-500-0

Foreign Intelligence Press is an independent,
privately owned publishing company and is not an
affiliate, subsidiary, or proprietary company of the
Central Intelligence Agency or any other intelligence organization or government agency.

Subsidiary rights inquiries to Stein and Day/*Publishers*, Scarborough House,
Briarcliff Manor, N.Y. 10510. This volume is distributed by Stein and
Day/*Publishers.*
ISBN 0-89568-500-0

Chief Advisors

RAY S. CLINE

Ray S. Cline, former Deputy Director for Intelligence of the CIA, began his intelligence career in 1942 by working in U.S. Navy codebreaking and then joining the OSS. Later he joined the CIA, in which he served as chief of station in Taiwan and Germany, and as Deputy Director for Intelligence during the Cuban missile crisis. From 1969 to 1973, he was the Director of the Bureau of Intelligence and Research in the U.S. Department of State.

Dr. Cline is founder and president of the National Intelligence Study Center in Washington, D.C. He is also senior advisor to the Center for Strategic and International Studies at Georgetown University and professor of international relations at Georgetown's School of Foreign Service.

Dr. Cline earned B.A., M.A., and Ph.D. degrees in history at Harvard University and was a Henry Prize Fellow at Oxford University's Balliol College. He has written or co-written 10 books on intelligence and strategic studies, including *Washington Command Post*, a reference work on military planning in World War II, and *The CIA under Reagan, Bush, and Casey*, which describes the American intelligence system since that war.

WALTER L. PFORZHEIMER

Walter L. Pforzheimer began his affiliation with intelligence in the U.S. Army Air Corps in 1942. From there, in 1946, he joined the newly formed Central Intelligence Group, continuing with its successor, CIA, until his retirement in 1974. From 1946 to 1956, he was the agency's Legislative Counsel, and in 1956 he established the CIA's Historical Intelligence Collection of books and other publications on all aspects of intelligence. In 1974 he was recalled as a consultant to the CIA general counsel and served until 1977. He also served on President-elect Ronald Reagan's CIA Transition Team in 1980-81.

Mr. Pforzheimer is a graduate of Yale University and Yale Law School, and in 1985 he received an honorary master of science of strategic intelligence degree from the Defense Intelligence College, where he is an adjunct professor.

An avid collector of books, Mr. Pforzheimer has the largest private collection of books and memorabilia on intelligence. He serves as an honorary trustee and advisor on special collections to the Yale University Library.

DAVID ATLEE PHILLIPS

David Atlee Phillips joined the CIA as a part-time agent in 1950 in Chile, where he was working as a newspaper editor. He became a full-time operative in 1954 and rose through the ranks to intelligence officer, chief of station, and eventually chief of all operations in the *Western Hemisphere*. He has served throughout Latin America, including Cuba, Mexico, Guatemala, and the Domincan Republic. He established his connection with intelligence during World War II, when as a prisoner of war in Germany he became a member of an escape committee, serving until his own escape.

In 1975, Mr. Phillips retired from the CIA to found the Association of Former Intelligence Officers (AFIO), an intelligence support group comprising 3,500 former intelligence officers from all services.

Mr. Phillips writes and lectures frequently on intelligence matters and is the author of five books, including *The Night Watch*, his CIA memoir, and *Careers in Secret Operations*, a guide to finding a job in the federal intelligence establishment. Currently, he is writing his sixth book, *History of CIA Directors and Covert Action*.

AUTHOR
JOHN PATRICK QUIRK

John Patrick Quirk, a publisher since 1967, has edited and written more than 100 social science books. For more than 12 years he was president and publisher of Special Learning International. His work in intelligence publishing stems from designing and publishing educational programs in Eastern and Western Europe and several third world countries, where Special Learning was the target of Soviet disinformation activities. He is currently writing a book tentatively titled *Soviet Active Measures in Book Publishing*.

Consultants

SAMUEL HALPERN

Samuel Halpern, a consultant on intelligence and national security, is a 32-year veteran of the OSS and CIA, where he became a senior officer. He graduated from City College of New York in 1942 and the National War College in 1966. Since 1975 he has served on the boards of directors of the Central Intelligence Retirees Association, the Association of Former Intelligence Officers, the National Intelligence Study Center, and the National Historical Intelligence Museum.

HANS MOSES

Hans Moses worked from 1953 to 1974 in the Clandestine Service of the CIA. After emigrating to the United States from his native Germany in 1939, he volunteered for infantry service with the U.S. Army. Once in Germany, however, he became an investigator-interrogator for army intelligence, thus beginning his career in intelligence. Shortly after the war, he became a civilian research analyst for the U.S. Air Force, serving there until he joined the CIA.

WILLIAM J. MULLIGAN

William J. Mulligan, director of operations for Varicon International, a security consulting firm, is a pathfinder in the development of technical intelligence collection capabilities, having set standards for and outlined improvements to modern collection technology. His distinguished career includes intelligence service in the State and Defense Departments as well as for the U.S. Army, Navy, and Air Force.

THOMAS POLGAR

Born in Hungary, Thomas Polgar emigrated to the United States, joined the OSS, and later rose to top positions in the CIA. He served as an intelligence officer and chief of station in Germany, Argentina, Mexico, and Vietnam. He distinguished himself and won the CIA's highest award for foiling a hijacking. He now writes on intelligence topics and is currently working on a book on the KGB.

HERBERT F. SAUNDERS

Herbert F. Saunders, president of Varicon International, served for many years in the CIA's Office of Technical Services (OTS), the office responsible for developing the tools and "gadgets" of intelligence. He achieved senior positions in OTS, including deputy director and chief of operations. Mr. Saunders also has an extensive background as a CIA security officer, and he is the recipient of the Distinguished Intelligence Medal.

THOMAS F. TROY

Thomas F. Troy, World War II veteran and former radio newscaster and college professor, spent 30 years working for the CIA. As an agency historian, he wrote *Donovan and the CIA: A History of the Establishment of the Central Intelligence Agency*, which was later published commercially, earning accolades as the definitive treatment of its subject. Mr. Troy, after his retirement, founded and was the first editor and principal writer of the Foreign Intelligence Literary Scene (FILS), a literary newsletter for "intelligencers." He is currently working on two books, one on the OSS and the other on Sir William Stephenson.

Interviews

RICHARD BISSELL
Former Director of Operations, CIA; developer of U-2, SR-71

LEO CHERNE
President, Research Institute of America; Vice-Chairman, President's Foreign Intelligence Advisory Board

WILLIAM E. COLBY
Former Director, Central Intelligence Agency

MAX CORVO
Former head of Secret Intelligence, OSS; President, OSS Symposium

DAVID ATLEE PHILLIPS
Former Chief of Western Hemisphere Operations, CIA

LIEUTENANT GENERAL EUGENE TIGHE
Former Director, Defense Intelligence Agency; President, Association of Former Intelligence Officers

ADMIRAL STANSFIELD TURNER
Former Director, Central Intelligence Agency

JAMES WITHROW
Attorney, Donovan, Leisure, Irvine and Newton, New York

I appreciate the many people who have commented, reviewed and permitted to be interviewed. Especially to Rev. Thomas Doyle of the Papal Nuncio's office, Washington, on the Vatican's intelligence, Senator Patrick Leahy of the Senate Intelligence Committee, Edward Sayle, preeminent intelligence historian and former CIA historian; Morton Halperin, Director, National Strategic Study Center, for his interview and comments on covert action; to the scores of OSS and CIA officers; to CIA family members; to John Greaney of the Association of Former Intelligence Officers; to A.J. Taylor and Larry McDonald of the National Archives; to all former DCI'S who I talked with; especially to Hon. John McCone, Hon. William Colby, Hon. Richard Helms, and Admiral Stansfield Turner.

I particularly appreciate the review and assistance by the following on specific materials:

Intelligence History: Walter Pforzheimer and Edward Sayle ; Donovan: Thomas Troy; OSS: Geoff Jones and the veterans of the OSS; Operations of the CIA, David Atlee Phillips and former station chiefs and case officers.

Intelligence Oversight: Leo Cherne, Admiral Turner and Morton Halperin, Senator Leahy and Daniel Finn;

The role of the KGB: to the former KGB officer who will go unnamed.

The former Chief of Station CIA who helped humanize material and who finally defined what a case officer and Chief of Station does.

I would also like to thank those intelligence officers of the British, Venezuelan and other services who were kind enough to review and support statements about CIA liaison and cooperation.

To the public affairs staff of the Central Intelligence Agency. Special appreciation to Mr. James Withrow of Donovan, Leisure, and Irvine who inspired me with OSS stories, Donovan anecdotes and helped set the basis and importance of General Donovan in creating the framework for CIA.

To Arelis Spencer who helped in a myriad of ways during the project.

I alone take responsibility for the content, photo captions, final changes, interviews, photos and artwork presented in this book.

John P. Quirk

Contents

FOREWORD
THE HONORABLE RICHARD HELMS

Nathan Hale, a young soldier-hero of the Revolutionary War, was one of our country's first intelligence officers. Hale is not remembered for his tradecraft, his professionalism. He was not trained for his assignment to obtain information on British military forces on Manhattan Island. He arrived too late to accomplish his mission, and the British found his secret writing instructions in his shoe before they executed him.

But I agree with a former colleague who has explained why intelligence officers revere Hale's memory: "Hale is what he is in the American pantheon not because of what he did, but because of why he did it."

It is apt that this volume about a modern intelligence institution should devote a significant number of its pages to early American clandestine operations and the freedom fighters who conducted them. Men like George Washington, who admonished an aide that "All that, remains for me to add is that you keep the whole matter secret ..." Men like Thomas Paine, who began one of his famous essays with the words' "If all men were angels ..."

If all men were angels this illustrated history of the Central Intelligence Agency would never have been published, as there would never have been a compelling reason for the establishment of the CIA. Indeed, if all men were angels the United States would need only token armed units rather than our world-wide military forces, and our vast police establishments could be replaced with constabularies.

But all men are not angels.

I have observed, as a foreign correspondent, naval officer, diplomat and, particularly, during three decades as an intelligence professional, that many nations of the world are governed by non-angels. While this state of affairs continues — and it appears unlikely it will change much in our lifetimes — we must have a CIA.

It is also fitting that this volume gives due note in its pages to General William Donovan's World War II Office of Strategic Services, the wartime intelligence organization where many of us who have served in the CIA learned our first lessons in clandestine operations.

The CIA was severely wounded in the mid-1970s by a series of investigations in which the internal workings of the Agency were scrutinized in public tribunals. Sensational headlines growing out of those investigations further lacerated our previously healthy organization. Some political commentators lamented the fact that the CIA was not the Boy Scouts. Those of us who worked in the CIA were surprised — we had always assumed that we had been expected to act otherwise. The CIA was damaged, almost crippled, by that dark period in its history.

Now the CIA has largely recuperated, and once again can serve American presidents and secretaries of state as it has in the past.

This volume will be useful to all Americans, especially young ones. It will help all citizens understand why we must protect our open society by conducting secret operations. It will remind us, as Nathan Hale did, that intelligence is necessary to the public good, and, by being necessary, becomes honorable.

These illustrations and these words not only describe what the CIA is but help explain why the CIA is what it is.

Richard M. Helms, 1986

PREFACE

Allen Dulles, a former Director of the Central Intelligence Agency, once referred to the CIA as "the bad boys of government." Director Richard Helms more recently stated, "This is neither a boy scout game nor a boxing bout fought by the Marquess of Queensberry rules. It's a job to be done." Since the agency's establishment in 1947, the media have reported consistently and fairly accurately of CIA involvement in the overthrow of governments, assassination plots, domestic spying, proprietary companies, paramilitary operations, the Bay of Pigs, the Cuban Missile Crisis, espionage operations, defectors, and other spying operations. This volume explores not only these sensational aspects of the CIA's clandestine services, but also its overt intelligence collection.

The unique aspect of the CIA is how it functions in a democracy. The CIA, one of the world's newest intelligence agencies, is also the most successful, because it does exactly what its charter states—gathers information in order that government leaders of the United States can make appropriate decisions on behalf of national security. An organization like the CIA must operate in strictest secrecy if it is to operate at all. Yet there are constant pressures from the media and other groups and from the public at large for the agency to divulge its secrets.

In almost all countries of the world, this volume would be prohibited by government decree or a nation's espionage laws. Even in certain Western democracies, intelligence cannot be discussed nor material published. Only in the United States, with our laws and freedoms, can a subject like the Central Intelligence Agency be discussed relatively openly.

This volume is an attempt to be an impartial chronicle of the Central Intelligence Agency, of its successes and failures, over the last 40 years.

PUBLISHER'S NOTE

When I decided to publish a photographic history of the Central Intelligence Agency, I discovered that former CIA staffers are not allowed to keep photos related to their work. I decided not to reproduce family photos offered to me by former CIA personnel as I felt it was an invasion of their privacy;

Another thing I discovered is that almost all photos of agency operations have simply disappeared.

Although I encountered no problems from CIA and no delays on clearances of manuscript from authors, I began to realize how difficult it was for those former CIA staffers to write in the 1970s on CIA. Obtaining photographs and information related to maps and graphics has proved equally difficult today.

Over the years very few photographs have been released by the CIA. Most photographs in stock agencies have disappeared, and these agencies even have been cleaned of glossy prints and of original negatives.

Personalities, buildings, photos of operations, and photos of key historical events have disappeared except for what is shown in this volume. A number of former CIA personnel have their own ideas on why they disappeared, and to where. Reliable and security-conscious photographic stock houses have no explanation.

Very little material exists on scientific and technological areas and tradecraft; tradecraft is almost impossible to document. Collectors who specialize are apt to want to believe they have an actual CIA weapon, CIA radio, CIA transmitter, and so forth, when in fact it is impossible to verify.

The security-conscious CIA has done an excellent job protecting its secrets, and the photographic area is no different. During our research, we have come across a number of excellent, never-released photo collections of KGB operations, many more than we were able to obtain on CIA. But this is the subject of our next volume: **The KGB—Soviet Intelligence, A Photographic History.**

John P. Quirk
Publisher

Introduction

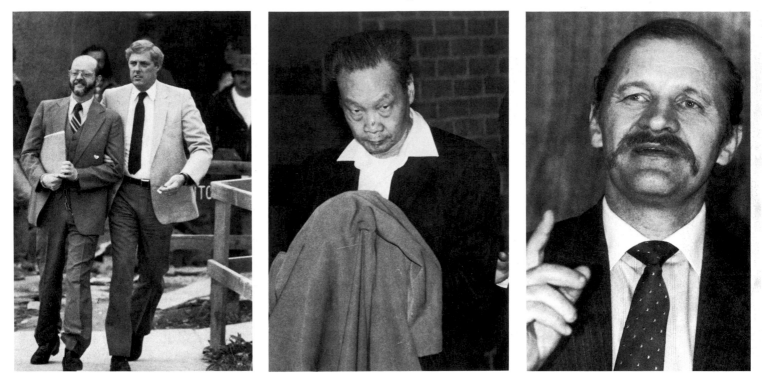

Spying for Money

CIA Officer Spied for Chinese for 30 Years!

Public and media interest in espionage and counterespionage resurged in 1985, a year that saw the revelation of one story after another about arrests, trials, and defections, both in the United States and abroad. But spying is not new. As long as people have been around, they have wanted to know what they were facing.

In more recent times, espionage took on a more ideological cloak. This is not to say that ideology has not been a factor before. But the war of ideas escalated with the development of communism and the violent emergence of the first Communist state, the Soviet Union, whose avowed goal was to export its revolution. Early on and particularly with the rise of Hitler in Germany, the Soviets were able to successfully recruit many leftist and liberal individuals. People with excellent educational backgrounds and impeccable social credentials were recruited; for example, Harold A.R. (Kim) Philby in England and Alger Hiss in the United States. The common thread linking the many disparate elements together into a popular front was their opposition to national socialism.

Once the war was over and the United States emerged as the Soviet Union's "main enemy," this popular front lost its appeal to most liberals in the United States and non-Communist leftists in Europe. No amount of Soviet propaganda could persuade the masses that America was a threat to the world. So the Soviets had to modify their approach. They realized that with the cold war now under way, their fellow Communists and sympathizers whose views were a matter of record would not get the clearances necessary for access to military, security, and defense secrets, no matter what their educational and social backgrounds. So they determined to recruit people who had access, regardless of their politics. But how to do this? In a capitalist society, money provided the answer.

Indeed, for more than 20 years, money has been the common motivator in the cases of Americans who were caught spying for the Soviet Union. It motivated Andrew Daulton Lee and Christopher Boyce, "the Falcon and the Snowman," to steal defense secrets from the TRW Corporation, an

Walker: Walter Mitty? or Spying for Dollars?

KGB Defector Redefects

American caught spying for Israelis

NSA employee accused of spying

FBI Agent Arrested For Spying

important defense contractor. It motivated Lieutenant Colonel William H. Whalen to provide the Soviets with information on nuclear weaponry, missiles, and other areas related to national defense and combat planning from the Strategic Air Command. And most recently, in 1985, it was the motivating factor in two particularly notorious cases: (1) that of Ronald W. Pelton, a former National Security Agency employee who admitted after his arrest that he sold U.S. intelligence secrets for more than five years; and (2) that of the Walker family—John, Arthur, Michael, and John's best friend Jerry Whitworth. When this spy ring was uncovered it was learned that John, who had recruited the others, had been selling navy secrets to the Soviets for more than 20 years.

Among many other cases that surfaced in 1985 in the U.S. are those of Edward Howard, a former CIA employee who reportedly was fingered as a Soviet spy by the on-again off-again defector Vitaly Yurchenko, whose redefection took many by surprise; and Larry Wu-Tai Chin, a CIA employee

who allegedly spied for the Peoples Republic of China for more than 30 years. The Department of Justice in November of that year announced that there was at that time a total of 36 espionage cases pending in U.S. courts, the greatest number ever.

From abroad came news of the defection to East Germany of Hans Joachim Tiedge, chief of the counterintelligence department of the West German Federal Security Agency; and the revelation that the KGB's chief of station in London had been working for Western intelligence for more than a decade.

All this activity has piqued public interest in espionage and in the organizations in charge of it. Hence the reason for this book. It is the publisher's intent to provide a relatively simple "explanation" of the Central Intelligence Agency, its methods, its reason for being, and in particular its history, for it is over the course of time that the CIA has evolved into what it is today: the foremost American intelligence organization and the most successful intelligence agency in the world.

The

Acme of Skill

The Mongol leader Subutai used men, women, and children to infiltrate his enemies' villages and armies to gather information. He was seldom defeated as a general and attributed his victories more to spying than to military prowess.

The

Hernando Cortes, always outnumbered, felt spying was essential to victory in his conquest of Mexico. He also used spies in the Spanish court and against the governor of Cuba (his immediate superior) to know their intentions. During his famous crossing of Mexico to attack the Aztec Indians, he received daily detailed reports of enemy troop dispositions, firepower, loyalty of allies, and agricultural stores. Cortes insisted on details and accuracy. Outnumbered by thousands of Indians, he believed good intelligence aided in recruiting allies and helped him plan military strategy.

The photo at right shows the *Return of the Spies* to Moses. The Israelites used spies frequently as the Israelis do today. Mossad, the intelligence agency for modern Israel is regarded as one of the best in the world.

Acme of Skill

The Acme of Skill

Intelligence gathering is not new. Espionage and intrigue were a tradition in Old World governments. The *art* of spying—and it is an art—court intrigue, and collecting information were common to the Phoenicians, Greeks, Romans, and other ancient civilizations. Although it is difficult to document before the Old Testament, it can be surmised that "knowing what the other fellow was up to" was important to one's security. In the Old Testament one reads that Moses was commanded by God to "spy out the Land of Canaan." Seeking and finding information was crucial to leaders of governments and their armies.

Four hundred years before the birth of Christ, the Chinese minister and military strategist, Sun Tzu, in his book, *The Art of War*, emphasized that the importance of good intelligence superseded war itself. Tzu stated, "To win 100 battles is not the acme of skill. To find security without fighting *is* the acme of skill."

Intelligence gathering was used in the 13th century by the Mongol leader Subutai in directing his forces to spectacular military successes in their invasion of Europe. It is safe to surmise that military and political intelligence gathering began in the Middle East or the Orient. As civilization and nation states developed, intelligence gathering developed simultaneously.

In the Western Hemisphere the Incas, Mayans, and Aztecs all had their spies and as a result strengthened their empires militarily. Hernando Cortes used spies—both Indian and Spanish—to better know the "attitude" and intentions of the Aztec ruler, Montezuma. Months before Cortes conquered Mexico, spies were preparing reports on the Aztecs' military preparedness, the loyalty of their allies, their economic resources, firepower, and the geographical area from the Gulf of Mexico to what is now Mexico City. History reveals that Asian, Middle Eastern, and American Indian rulers also gave intelligence gathering top priority.

Allen Dulles, regarded as one of the best American spymasters, was from America's elite, well educated, brilliant, and an early director of the Office of Strategic Services in Switzerland during World War II. After the war he served as Director of the Central Intelligence Agency for more than nine years. Well respected by CIA agents and staff, he served during the early years of the cold war. He took much of the blame for the Bay of Pigs planning and debacle. As a result he was relieved by President John F. Kennedy in 1961. His many contributions to America's intelligence capabilities are still being felt today.

Cardinal Richelieu, leader, man of the Church, politician, and spymaster. Richelieu helped France achieve great power. The days of swashbuckling musketeers, court intrigue, spying, and counterespionage are well documented from historical papers. Some of these records are the first European documents recorded about espionage and some of the first known by the general public. Alexandre Dumas, in writing *The Three Musketeers*, is said to have drawn on these papers for his famous story.

Allen Welsh Dulles, Director of the Central Intelligence Agency for nine years, wrote in his superb book, *The Craft of Intelligence*, that European rulers during the Middle Ages "were not very well informed about the Byzantine Empire and the Eastern Slavs; they knew even less about the Moslem world; and they were almost completely ignorant of anything that went on in Central and East Asia." Later, however, the European leaders used spying as an accepted policy of their governments' state departments. Their reasons were similar to the reasons of nations today—the need for military preparedness, for economic and trade information, and to gain knowledge of the adversary's scientific achievements.

Court intrigue, spying, and extensive subversive operations multiplied during the time of Leonardo da Vinci, Machiavelli, the Borgias, and the Renaissance papacy. In France in the 17th century, Cardinal Richelieu had his spies in the Vatican and in England.

Richelieu believed that the grandeur of France was dependent on sound information that would help him control the political affairs of Europe. In the 16th century, Sir Francis Walsingham, principal State Secretary to Queen Elizabeth I of England, developed a network of dozens of foreign intelligence agents. He dispatched them throughout Europe and the Middle East. He recruited most of the agents from Cambridge and Oxford. Their qualifications were the ability to speak foreign languages, live abroad without assistance from their governments, and be adept at penetration of other governments. He trained them in covert activities, taught them codebreaking and other skills. In these first well-documented examples, Walsingham established the aspects of the first modern intelligence organization.

NICCOLÖ MACCHIAVELLI

Machiavelli, in his famous writings, especially *The Prince*, set the standard for espionage philosophy. Machiavelli in writing about deceit stressed: show a friendly face even if you don't mean it; act the opposite in front of enemies, using deception but never letting your enemy know —show a friendly face. Machiavelli's philosophy showed that espionage was a game and in playing the game one must hide his true feelings.

The art of intelligence is not new. It was practiced during the reign of Queen Elizabeth I of England (1558–1603).

Sir Francis Walsingham, Elizabeth's principal State Secretary, created an extensive intelligence organization that sent agents to foreign lands. Today, the British Secret Service is regarded as one of the top intelligence agencies in the world.

New World

This historical map illustrates the claims and ambitions of the French and English in North America. Spying both in the New World and in Europe increased as the stakes for land, wealth, and power increased.

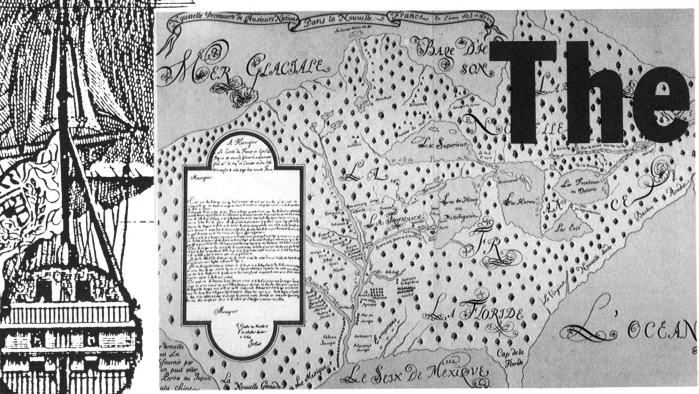

New World

The New World

When the first immigrants arrived on American shores the art of spying had already been developed in the courts of England, France, Spain, Portugal, Holland, Italy, Germany, Russia, and Belgium. Many of these immigrants hoped to leave behind religious persecution, poverty, and the intrigues of courts and find economic opportunity and freedom in America.

Most of the first settlers on the east coast came from England, Scotland, Ireland, and France; on the west coast they came from Spain.

The European governments transferred their ambitions for power to the New World. Spying against one another became an integral part of colonial policy. The French resented English expansion into the territories of North America where the French were exploring, fur trapping, and trading. The English felt the same way about French interests in areas like Canada and along the Mississippi and when the French established forts as far west as Detroit and Chicago. Both feared the Spanish, who had conquered and settled Florida, most of Latin America, the Caribbean, Mexico, and what is now the southwestern United States. Thus, gathering information about each other's activities was of top importance.

The English coveted all of North America. The French and English used American Indians, who lived all over the continent, as spies. The Indians, knowing the land and the cultures of other tribes, became ideal agents—especially when rewarded with liquor, guns, and trinkets. Tribes became loyal to the English or French, often as an excuse to defend themselves against other tribes.

The Spanish, more isolated and with their possessions spread over thousands of miles, usually came

British seapower was strengthened by espionage and intelligence gathering. This Spanish ship (left) was attacked and sunk off the coast of Venezuela. English spies in Caracas sent word through Trinidad that the ship was laden with gold and military stores.

into contact with the English in the Caribbean. A "gentlemen's agreement" gave Cuba, Santo Domingo, the Bahamas, Puerto Rico, and other islands to the Spanish; the French occupied Haiti, Martinique, and a few others. The British moved into Jamaica, Bermuda, and Trinidad and began trying to take control of the Bahamas and other islands. Spying became mostly naval intelligence. Watching shipping, troop movements, and the construction of forts were the major concerns. Naval intelligence helped many a British ship intercept and capture or sink Spanish galleons loaded with gold. The English also sacked and looted Spanish cities from the Caribe to Maracaibo, Venezuela.

On the North American continent it was quite different. The Spanish were content to control most of Latin America as far north as Mexico and what is now California, Texas, New Mexico, and Arizona, the terri-tories of the southwest—until these territories were eventually wrested from them by the upstart United States. The French and English during the 15th to 17th centuries were on the east coast—a continent away and no serious threat. The only threat to the Spanish in the 17th century was the Russians, who were colonizing Alaskan territories and eyeing Oregon and California. Intelligence from the European courts informed the Spanish that the Russian bear was on the move but did not have the resources to seize control of California from Spain.

Throughout the 16th and 17th centuries the French and English continued their longstanding animosity. The new settlers in America became unwilling participants in these conflicts, especially during the French and Indian War. The French used Indians to attack British troops and American settlers. Both sides used Indians as spies and combatants. Captain

The early settlers used Indians to spy against other rival colonial powers. The French, English, and Spanish all had their own lists of loyal tribes.

"Roger's Rangers" were the first of the "elite" forces used in the Americas. Today the United States has a number of elite forces used in support, as part of, or as "liaison" with CIA operations. These include the 82nd Airborne, the Delta Force, Special Forces Green Berets, Army Rangers, U.S. Marines, Navy Seals, and "top secret" forces. With the increase in terrorism it is likely the emphasis and training of more "elite" units will be necessary. The military and the intelligence community is split on whether CIA operations should be involved with covert military actions.

Rogers, the American commander of the "Rangers," used Indians to obtain information and attack the Abanaki Indians who had been massacring American settlers and raiding American forts. During these early days of New World settlements, most intelligence was of a military nature and was based on the aspirations for conquest of the British and French. Usually, the average American was more concerned about his daily life of farming, trading, shipbuilding and seafaring. As hopes for independence loomed, the Founding Fathers of the United States began to see the necessity of knowing as much as possible about English intentions in the 13 colonies.

From the 16th century to the present, recorded history demonsrates that the survival of nations has depended on more than large armies. They have survived by their ability to gather, evaluate, and understand information about their world. Just as an

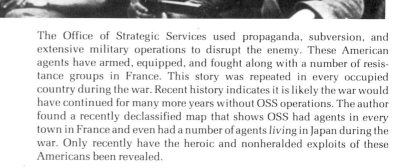

The Office of Strategic Services used propaganda, subversion, and extensive military operations to disrupt the enemy. These American agents have armed, equipped, and fought along with a number of resistance groups in France. This story was repeated in every occupied country during the war. Recent history indicates it is likely the war would have continued for many more years without OSS operations. The author found a recently declassified map that shows OSS had agents in every town in France and even had a number of agents *living* in Japan during the war. Only recently have the heroic and nonheralded exploits of these Americans been revealed.

attorney must collect facts before he can defend his client or a loan officer must research a person's credit in order to determine his worthiness for a loan, nations have to collect information to plan strategy. Mata Hari, of World War I fame, the courageous American OSS agents who parachuted into German-occupied France during World War II, and the atomic spies of the 1950s all had more or less the same goal—to obtain information for their side. This evaluated information is intelligence.

Forewarned Is Forearmed

During World War II, American fears of Hitler's "super weapons" almost came true when it was discovered Hitler's scientists were rapidly develop-

Partly completed Heinkel 162s, single-jet planes with a speed of 650 miles per hour. These planes were found by OSS and 9th Army units. In early 1945, Hitler accelerated production, still hoping to defeat Allied air forces. This plant, found 300 meters beneath the ground at Engels, Germany, produced 50 planes per day. A large elevator brought the completed planes to the surface.

ing the jet airplane, the intercontinental ballistic missile, and the atomic bomb. Hitler, some experts theorize, was but months away from having the capability of mass producing atomic bombs that could be delivered by missiles able to hit New York and jet airplanes that could drop bombs on Allied armies in England, France, and Russia.

Today, the microchip age has spawned technological nonhuman spies as well as human "scientific" field agents. The importance of advancing "super" technology in the area of microcomputers, space stations, "killer" satellites, and "super" nuclear weapons has accelerated the race for information gathering. The "Star Wars" proposal of the Reagan administration has set the Soviet KGB—Soviet Intelligence Service—scurrying to learn secret American technology.

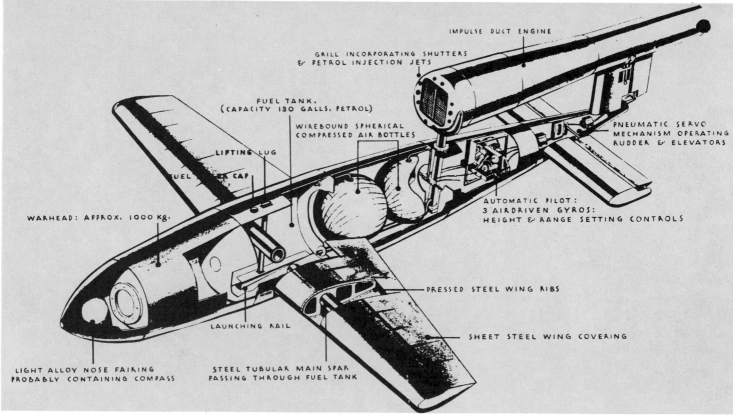

IMPULSE DUCT ENGINE

GRILL INCORPORATING SHUTTERS
& PETROL INJECTION JETS

FUEL TANK,
(CAPACITY 130 GALLS. PETROL)

WIREBOUND SPHERICAL
COMPRESSED AIR BOTTLES

PNEUMATIC SERVO
MECHANISM OPERATING
RUDDER & ELEVATORS

LIFTING LUG

FUEL FILL CAP

AUTOMATIC PILOT:
3 AIRDRIVEN GYROS:
HEIGHT & RANGE SETTING CONTROLS

WARHEAD: APPROX. 1000 Kg.

PRESSED STEEL WING RIBS

LAUNCHING RAIL

SHEET STEEL WING COVERING

LIGHT ALLOY NOSE FAIRING
PROBABLY CONTAINING COMPASS

STEEL TUBULAR MAIN SPAR
PASSING THROUGH FUEL TANK

Today the nations that have nuclear weapons number five. By the end of the century it is expected that ten nations will have nuclear weapons. The Soviet Union obtained its first nuclear capability through espionage and an aggressive intelligence service. For new, developing countries nuclear weaponry can be had by known science or stealing secrets and the materials needed to make "the bomb." In addition, the major intelligence services have all reported the movement by terrorist groups to develop a bomb.

This cutaway view of a German flying bomb shows the intricate workings of the first missiles. German engineers were in the final stages of developing intercontinental missiles able to hit New York. At the end of the war the Nazis were accelerating this project along with the planning of nuclear devices.

British soldiers examine a V-2 rocket found near a chemical factory in the German forest of Hannenberg. Hitler hoped that rockets like the V-2 equipped with explosives and even chemical weapons would turn near defeat into victory.

Hitler ordered rapid production of flying bombs like the one seen here. He hoped that eventually, atomic bombs would be used.

The attack on Pearl Harbor on December 7, 1941, is the main reason that the United States formed one, central intelligence agency. The development of the atomic bomb by other nations and the increase in nuclear development by terrorist groups are thought by many intelligence experts to be reasons to strengthen the CIA.

MRBM LAUNCH SITE 1
SAN CRISTOBAL, CUBA
23 OCTOBER 1962

MISSILE ERECTOR

CABLE

MISSILE SHELTER TENT

TRACKED PRIME MOVERS

NUCLEAR WARHEAD BUNKER UNDER CONSTRUCTION
SAN CRISTOBAL SITE 1

These now famous photos of Soviet missile bases in Cuba were obtained by photo reconnaissance. Human agents, the Cuban underground, and a Soviet defector all played an important part in supplying President Kennedy with good intelligence—intelligence that caused Premier Khrushchev to lie, get caught in his lie, and eventually back down and remove the missiles.

The need to keep secret and know information is and has always been necessary to a nation's security. Whether the information is obtained from an American satellite or a Soviet trade delegate seeking American "know-how" the needs are crucial. They are more crucial today for two major reasons: 1. more nations today have nuclear weapons and more are obtaining them; 2. the world's superpowers, a la the "Star Wars" scenario, fear that one nation may develop the ultimate super weapon or develop some type of technology capable of dominating their opposite number.

More and more nations (and, possibly, terrorist groups) are developing the capability to build nuclear bombs, and more technology is being developed to "get the jump" on other nations. Simply put, intelligence is knowledge and foreknowledge of the world that surrounds us. The art of delivering this knowledge in a fashion that allows decision-makers to arrive at a proper decision is difficult and challenging to any intelligence service. The collection of facts, the analysis, collating, sorting, organizing, digesting and scrutinizing of them requires more than the cloak-and-dagger activities of moviemakers. Intelligence must be rigorous, continuous, timely, and useful. The combination of informing and alerting is what intelligence is all about. In today's media-oriented world of computers, television, cinema, books, radio, and volatile changing "future shock" situations, that combination is essential and an absolute necessity. Without it, nations would have to live on faith alone—or be totally in the dark. This combination could have helped avoid Pearl Harbor and, in the future, might avoid a second Cuban missile crisis, and perhaps World War III.

The Papacy

The Papacy

Since early times, the Roman Catholic church has needed information and intelligence. When the church was first struggling to survive within the structure of a repressive regime from Rome, intelligence was a matter of survival. The early Christians were apprehended and executed as a matter of course. As the doctrines of Christ spread, the organization and power of the church spread as well. Early intelligence gathering for survival was soon replaced by intelligence gathering to keep popes informed of the loyalty of cardinals and countries. Since most of Europe became Catholic, it was necessary for the pope to maintain his power through the loyalty of the faithful. Intelligence gathering was conducted by Vat-

ican clergy and nobles loyal to the pope. These agents reported on matters of dogma, financial collections, and obedience to papal orders. As the church spread and its financial and political powers developed, intelligence gathering became part and parcel of daily operations.

During the Inquisition, spies from the Vatican reported on the heretics as well as the conduct of the inquisitors. During the Protestant Reformation spies from the papacy flourished. With the influence of the Borgias and the Avignon papacy (a separate French papacy) both popes spied on each other. The Roman connection won out and consolidated its hold on the church worldwide. Today, most intelligence gathering conducted by the church is based on its ability to

THE
ROMAN CATHOLIC
CHURCH

Number of Roman Catholics	900,000,000
Number of parishes	360,000
Number of orders	450
Number of universities, hospitals, and institutions	300,000
Number of priests and clergy	2,000,000

Vatican Wealth

Art collections	Priceless, but worth billions
Productive investments	$125 million to $185 million
Vatican Bank	$3 billion in assets
Real estate	Trillions of dollars
Daily/monthly contributions	Classified
Peter's Pence contributions	Classified
Other assets, such as companies, insurance, loans owed	Billions

Source: *Forbes* Magazine and the Vatican

Like any nation, the Vatican must collect intelligence to function well. In centuries past, when much of the known Western world was Catholic, the popes needed information to control their empire. Today, the Vatican uses intelligence to formulate policy for the church worldwide and to provide security for, among other things, its vast wealth.

flourish in countries not wholly friendly to religion. The official policy of the church has always been against Marxist Soviet and Communistic expansion and ideology, although in Latin America a number of priests and nuns appear to engage in pro-Communist activities. The hierarchy in Rome frowns on this. Its official position is to keep clear of political situations. This is often very difficult because in many countries the power clique is composed of the clergy.

The intelligence network, even when it is informal, provides the pope with important information necessary to policy in various countries. The policy of Pope John Paul II in relation to Poland and his outspoken criticism of the Soviet Union is one major reason the Bulgarian secret police and the Soviet Union's KGB are suspected of the assassination attempt on his life. The Roman Catholic church is an ally to those who oppose communism and the church is also an intelligence source important to countries that oppose communism.

American Intelligence

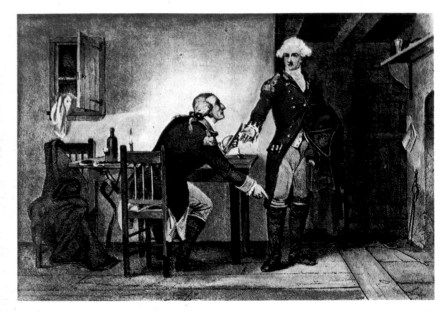

The illustration above shows Benedict Arnold—traitor and spy. Arnold was a major general in the American army. He became a traitor because he felt his achievements were not recognized. He is shown here with Major John André, who was executed for spying. Arnold died in disgrace. André who had designed ladies clothing and coiffures, was executed by the Americans after patriots found papers in his boots.

American

General George Washington needed spies for his fledgling Continental Army. Being out-gunned and with British troops posted all over the United States, Washington needed to rely on spies.

Edmund Burke, pictured at right, was followed and his mail opened by British agents who feared Burke had close ties to American revolutionaries.

Intelligence

The American Revolution

American intelligence gathering began during the Revolutionary War. American and English spies engaged in political and military espionage in the colonies and in Europe. George Washington assigned spies Major Benjamin Tallmadge and Captain Nathan Hale to gather intelligence. Spies for the English were Tories, Indians, and their own men. The Tories or Loyalists, as they were called in America, believed England would easily defeat the American patriots and thus spied on their own neighbors. After America achieved independence the Tories suffered confiscations of property and some went voluntarily to Canada and England. The Tories collaborated by going through enemy lines, passing coded messages, reporting on American troop strength and morale, and even committing sabotage. The most notorious English spy was an American general—Benedict Arnold—perhaps the first double agent in American

history. He was certainly the first defector. Arnold's name has become synonymous with traitor. Arnold almost caused a tremendous setback to Washington where he tried to turn over West Point to the British before his "controller," the British agent Major John André, was executed by the Americans.

Military information was crucial to George Washington who, understaffed and outgunned, needed stealth and brains to outwit and defeat a superior British army. His need for spies increased during the war. The other "front" for espionage was Europe. American delegates were sent to Europe to enlist the aid of France and other countries unfriendly to England. Benjamin Franklin was spied on by British agents interested in knowing how serious the French were in helping the Americans. In England, Edmund Burke and other members of Parliament sympathetic to the American cause had their mail opened and

The above cartoon shows the British burning the White House during the War of 1812.

Tories—those colonists loyal to England—are shown being driven out of the United States. After the war—largely because of their spying activities—they were forced to flee to Canada, England, and elsewhere. The photo at left shows a Tory spy being driven out of New York to Canada.

Benjamin Franklin was involved in spying in France during the Revolution. British agents also kept track of his movements and especially of any new developments that might bring France into the war on the side of the Americans.

were followed and harassed by British "special agents."

Although most of the spying was of a military or political nature, it was to affect the economies of all nations. The new nation finally enlisted the aid of the French and finally achieved independence. Recent historians believe that without French money and military support the new nation might not have been established. After the War of Independence not many Americans saw the need for an army, let alone an intelligence gathering group. Thus, no intelligence force was considered, although from time to time individuals performed "special missions" for the President or the Department of State.

The next century in American history saw the need for military preparedness more than intelligence gathering for economic or scientific information. Thus, most intelligence came from the navy or army. Although the United States expanded tremendously from 1800 to 1900, the need for military intelligence

In this portrait of the burning of Washington in 1814 British agents carrry off "intelligence" papers of the Americans.

Many historians believe that if the defenders of the Alamo had better intelligence they could have reinforced the Alamo or delayed the Mexican attack.

was based on the wars in which America became involved. After the Revolutionary War, the United States fought the War of 1812 against the British. Information gathering was further complicated in those days by the delays in communications. The Battle of New Orleans occurred some two weeks after a peace treaty was concluded. Although it is difficult to imagine how intelligence gathering could have stopped the battle, it is interesting to speculate whether the sacking and burning of the White House by British troops could have been prevented if the United States had developed better intelligence.

Army intelligence did serve the nation well later— during the Mexican War, when troops landed at Vera Cruz, stormed Chapultepec, and marched into Mexico City. Even during the longstanding Indian Wars the Army used Indians to spy on other Indians. This was not as successful as anticipated, however, because the code of most of the Plains Indians prohibited this kind of clandestine behavior.

The Civil War increased espionage both in the U.S. and abroad and on land, sea, and even in the air. The photo above shows the observation and spy balloon, *Intrepid*. Later, the famous British spymaster—Sir William Stephenson—used the codename Intrepid in working with the Office of Strategic Services—forerunner to the Central Intelligence Agency.

Harriet Tubman, famous as a slave smuggler, also spied for the Union—making scores of trips through Southern lines.

The Civil War

During the Civil War spying became a top priority for both sides. Aerial balloons were used by the Union to locate troop dispositions. The navy employed spies in England to keep an eye on the laird-ram ships constructed by the English for use by Confederates against Union shipping. Spies were also used to determine how sympathetic the English and French were to the Confederacy. Lincoln wanted to keep England and other countries from diplomatically recognizing and aiding the Confederacy. Both spies and *agents provaceteurs* travelled between the lines. Harriet Tubman the famous Negro slave smuggler also spied and carried information for the Union. Confederate intelligence could never truly gain knowledge of Union industrial strength however, and was hampered by Lincoln's blockade.

After the war, minor intelligence gathering was continued but not really needed. Very few Americans except the well educated, spoke or read foreign lan-guages or knew the cultures of other lands. Moreover, the location of the United States helped serve as a defense and a barrier to outside interference.

Would better intelligence have prevented the Spanish from sinking the *Maine*? Although there is controversy over the cause of the USS *Maine* explosion—was it an accident or did the Spanish sink it—our ability to spy against the Spanish was limited. Most members of our diplomatic corps spoke only English. Moreover, most military dispatches were coded and almost impossible for Americans to break. The United States just did not have an organized intelligence gathering force. During the war, the destruction of the Spanish fleet resulted from information supplied by naval intelligence. As the United States expanded its influence, it became apparent that better intelligence gathering was needed. However, a formal service was not considered. Even though the United States was becoming a world power and had

THE LIFE OF A SPY—IN NINE TABLEAUX.

IN THE ENEMY'S WORKS.

SUSPECTED

WHO GOES THERE.

THE LIFE OF A SPY.

BOOTY.

SAFE RETURN.

IN PURSUIT.

SENTENCE

TELLING HIS ADVENTURES.

American public interest in spying began during the Civil War. These prints show some of the glamour, the duties, and an unfortunate end of a Civil War spy.

The photo at left shows the hanging of rebel spies, Williams and Peters, in 1863 by the Army of the Cumberland.

The defeat of the Spanish fleet in Manila Bay was the result of good naval intelligence.

Homer Lea was one of the first Americans to do intelligence work in China. He travelled with Sun Yat-sen and reported back to America on how to establish intelligence networks. Clare Boothe Luce discovered his writings and had them published.

possessions in Cuba, the Phillipines, Hawaii and Puerto Rico, many Americans thought we should stay out of European conflicts. America was isolated from Europe and Asia by oceans and Canada and Mexico were friendly nations. No troops were garrisoned on our borders. Moreover, the Monroe Doctrine helped keep Europeans from the Western Hemisphere. They were not interested in a conflict with the United States. Besides, spying was regarded by most Americans as unworthy and unbecoming a nation that prided itself on its Bill of Rights, its freedoms, and its independence. For these reasons and a strong isolationist sentiment the American army remained small. Only the United States Navy, because of Theodore Roosevelt's efforts, expanded. For the majority of the country's political and military leaders, spying was not necessary. Spying "was not done by gentlemen" and the accepted belief was that it really was not necessary.

$50,000 REWARD.—WHO DESTROYED THE MAINE?—$50,000 REWARD.

EDITION FOR GREATER NEW YORK

NEW YORK JOURNAL
AND ADVERTISER.

The Journal will give $50,000 for information, furnished to it exclusively, that will convict the person or persons who sank the Maine.

The Journal will give $50,000 for information, furnished to it exclusively, that will convict the person or persons who sank the Maine.

NO. 5,572. Copyright, 1898, by W. R. Hearst—NEW YORK, THURSDAY, FEBRUARY 17, 1898.—16 PAGES. PRICE ONE CENT In Greater New York | Elsewhere and Jersey City. | TWO CENTS.

DESTRUCTION OF THE WAR SHIP MAINE WAS THE WORK OF AN ENEMY.

$50,000!
$50,000 REWARD!
For the Detection of the Perpetrator of the Maine Outrage!

The New York Journal hereby offers a reward of $50,000 CASH for information. FURNISHED TO IT EXCLUSIVELY, which shall lead to the detection and conviction of the person, persons or government criminally responsible for the explosion which resulted in the destruction, at Havana, of the United States war ship Maine and the loss of 258 lives of American sailors.

The $50,000 CASH offered for the above information is on deposit with Wells, Fargo & Co.

No one is barred, be he the humble but misguided seaman eking out a few miserable dollars by acting as a spy, or the attache of a government secret service, plotting by any devilish means, to revenge fancied insults or cripple menacing countries.

This offer has been cabled to Europe and will be made public in every capital of the Continent and in London this morning.

The Journal believes that any man who can be bought to commit murder can also be bought to betray his comrades. FOR THE PERPETRATOR OF THIS OUTRAGE HAD ACCOMPLICES.

W. R. HEARST.

Assistant Secretary Roosevelt Convinced the Explosion of the War Ship Was Not an Accident.

The Journal Offers $50,000 Reward for the Conviction of the Criminals Who Sent 258 American Sailors to Their Death. Naval Officers Unanimous That the Ship Was Destroyed on Purpose.

$50,000!
$50,000 REWARD!
For the Detection of the Perpetrator of the Maine Outrage!

The New York Journal hereto offers a reward of $50,000 CASH for information FURNISHED TO IT EXCLUSIVELY, which shall lead to the detection and conviction of the person, persons or government criminally responsible for the explosions which resulted in the destruction, at Havana, of the United States war ship Maine and the loss of 258 lives of American sailors.

The $50,000 CASH offered for the above information is on deposit with Wells, Fargo & Co.

No one is barred, be he the humble, but misguided, seaman, eking out a few miserable dollars by acting as a spy, or the attache of a government secret service, plotting by any devilish means, to revenge fancied insults or cripple menacing countries.

This offer has been cabled to Europe and will be made public in every capital of the Continent and in London this morning.

The Journal believes that any man who can be bought to commit murder can also be bought to betray his comrades. FOR THE PERPETRATOR OF THIS OUTRAGE HAD ACCOMPLICES.

W. R. HEARST.

POWDER MAGAZINE

NAVAL OFFICERS THINK THE MAINE WAS DESTROYED BY A SPANISH MINE.

George Eugene Bryson, the Journal's special correspondent at Havana, cables that it is the secret opinion of many Spaniards in the Cuban capital that the Maine was destroyed and 258 of her men killed by means of a submarine mine, or fixed torpedo. This is the opinion of several American naval authorities. The Spaniards, it is believed, arranged to have the Maine anchored over one of the harbor mines. Wires connected the mine with a powder magazine, and it is thought the explosion was caused by sending an electric current through the wire. If this can be proven, the brutal nature of the Spaniards will be shown by the fact that they waited to spring the mine until after all the men had retired for the night. The Maltese cross in the picture shows where the mine may have been fired.

Hidden Mine or a Sunken Torpedo Believed to Have Been the Weapon Used Against the American Man-of-War---Officers and Men Tell Thrilling Stories of Being Blown Into the Air Amid a Mass of Shattered Steel and Exploding Shells---Survivors Brought to Key West Scout the Idea of Accident---Spanish Officials Protest Too Much---Our Cabinet Orders a Searching Inquiry---Journal Sends Divers to Havana to Report Upon the Condition of the Wreck.
Was the Vessel Anchored Over a Mine?
BY CAPTAIN E. L. ZALINSKI, U. S. A.
(Captain Zalinski is the inventor of the famous dynamite gun, which would be the principal factor in our coast defence in case of war.)

Assistant Secretary of the Navy Theodore Roosevelt says he is convinced that the destruction of the Maine in Havana Harbor was not an accident. The Journal offers a reward of $50,000 for exclusive evidence that will convict the person, persons or Government criminally responsible for the destruction of the American battle ship and the death of 258 of its crew.

The suspicion that the Maine was deliberately blown up grows stronger every hour. Not a single fact to the contrary has been produced.

Captain Sigsbee, of the Maine, and Consul-General Lee both urge that public opinion be suspended until they have completed their investigation. They are taking the course of tactful men who are convinced that there has been treachery.

Washington reports very late that Captain Sigsbee had feared some such event as a hidden mine. The English cipher code was used all day yesterday by the naval officers in cabling instead of the usual American code.

The newspaper depicted above expresses public sentiment about the explosion of the *Maine*. The bottom of the article indicates the early use of codes and also the poor coordination of intelligence.

39

At right is a photo of Colonel William Donovan (1917) commander of the "Fighting 69th," an Irish-American army regiment during World War I. Donovan was said to begin thinking about "a central intelligence agency" as early as World War I. He was impressed with British intelligence and foresaw America's growing role as a world power. In 1981 the CIA admitted that Donovan had intelligence training in Europe during World War I. The extent, however, was probably very limited as Donovan was busy as a commander, participated in a number of battles, and won scores of other medals, including the Medal of Honor—America's highest military award.

World War

World War I began to change these attitudes. First, propaganda by both the British and Germans started to impact on America. The English wanted American help and the Germans wanted the United States to stay out of the conflict. The United States really became an impartial observer and did little to monitor foreign agents in the country. There was no FBI, and the United States still had a very small military force. When America did enter the war most intelligence gathering was haphazard and of a military nature. The United States had no idea of the number of spies in the country or their efforts to influence politicians and the general public. As in the Civil War the American public began to read about spying related to the war. The most celebrated spy was the Dutch-born German spy Mata Hari, an exceptionally beautiful woman, but a very poor agent. British Secret Service agents also became the heroes of the American public with their exploits in Europe, the Mideast, and Asia (chronicled

William Donovan (center) seated in front of his tent near McAllen, Texas, during the Mexican crisis in 1916.

After the U.S. declared war on Germany, William Donovan volunteered to serve as an officer in the historic Fighting 69th. To keep his men in shape he led them on long, grueling runs, earning the sobriquet of "Wild Bill."

probably by the British themselves) and relayed to American journalists and publishing houses. The British had in fact set up agents in every country and had extensive counterintelligence and covert operations.

As allies, the British were still not willing to share any intelligence information and thus the Americans started to realize the importance of such a service. One such American was William "Wild Bill" Donovan. Donovan was a commander of the "Fighting 69th"—the Rainbow Division. The "Fighting 69th" was largely made up of Irish-Americans who fought in a number of significant World War I battles. Donovan was a much admired leader, a brave commander who won a score of medals, was wounded, and was awarded the Congressional Medal of Honor. The poet Joyce Kilmer, who was killed during the war, Father Duffy, and others became legendary heroes.

After the war the United States became firmly

The above photos show (top to bottom) a Rollin Kirby cartoon commenting on the mass roundups, jailings, and deportations of aliens; Attorney General Mitchell Palmer, led the "Red" hunts; aliens waiting deportation.

When the Soviets took control of Russia Lenin established the Cheka (1921) to conduct purges and establish foreign intelligence. This was greatly expanded into the GPU, also established by Lenin. The NKVD was formed in 1934 with even broader police and espionage duties. Stalin used the NKVD to arrest and execute political opponents who he usually accused of working for foreign intelligence services. Today the Soviets have the KGB and GRU, and they control their client states' intelligence services. Besides having the same police powers as their predecessor the NKVD, the KGB controls border guards, immigration, and intelligence, and they have become experts at disinformation and stealing American technology. Their goals for the 1980s are to plant "deep cover" agents in the United States and to cause American intelligence to go on wild goose chases investigating American citizens and each other's intelligence agencies.

entrenched in isolationism and wanted no part of Europe. The United States was becoming pre-occupied with Prohibition, the Red Scares, and later, the Great Depression. During the Red Scares of the 1920s, most so-called foreign agents and "Reds" were arrested on very little evidence and jailed or deported to their country of origin. Their lot was further hindered by the lack of an FBI or CIA to determine the seriousness and extent of Communist or subversive activities. The Red Scares fueled distrust of terms like anarchy, spies, revolution, and Europe. Americans associated spies with bearded conspirators plotting to overthrow the government. The country wanted no association with such "foreign" ideas.

During these days of isolationism, the Soviet Union, first under the leadership of Lenin, then Stalin, already paranoid about its security, broadened its intelligence gathering capabilities by expanding its intelligence service—the Cheka. It actually made it part of the Communist government and employed

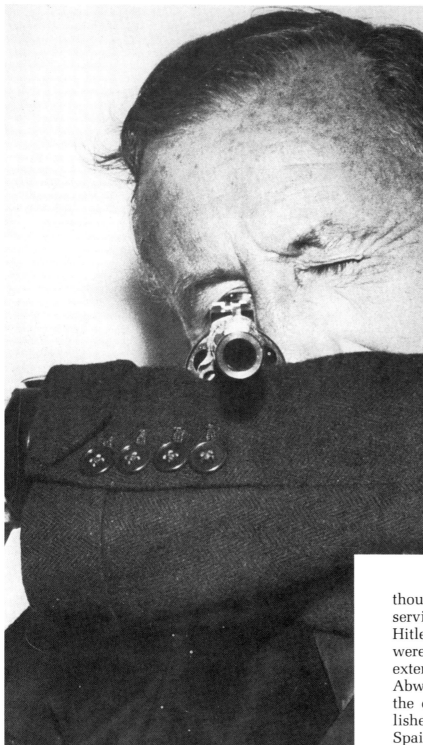

The "real James Bond"? Ian Fleming, who wrote the most successful spy novels—over 50 million copies in print—was in fact involved in intelligence operations before and after the war. Fleming served as liaison to Sir William Stephenson in New York and Washington, claimed to have actually written the draft and plan for organizing American intelligence in early 1941 (with William Donovan), and did in fact carry on some of the exploits in his 007 books. Whether he or Dusko Popov was the model for James Bond, most CIA staffers scoff at the Bond exploits.

thousands for spying. The British and French security services also expanded. When Mussolini in Italy and Hitler in Germany came to power, their first steps were to establish secret police forces for internal and external spying. The German Gestapo and the Abwehr (military intelligence) were later joined by the dreaded SS. The other nations that had established intelligence services were Japan, Mexico, Spain, Portugal, Austria, Serbia (later Yugoslavia), and Turkey. The United States had none.

Even though the British government did not take action against Hitler, the British Secret Service saw the war clouds gathering and accelerated its intelligence gathering. One such move was to locate Sir William Stephenson in the United States. Stephenson, a Canadian businessman and former World War I pilot, located offices in New York before World War II. His mission was to bring America into the war on England's side or help steer the United States into neutrality.

The photo shows a scene from the Pearl Harbor attack. Although the American military had broken the Japanese code, poor coordination delayed the information and resulted in the attack with the unsuspecting Americans losing over 2,300 lives. Pearl Harbor has become the rallying event for intelligence experts who hope that another such disaster never happens to the United States.

Fighting fires on the battleship USS *West Virginia*. Poor intelligence coordination hurt the United States in defending against the attack. Breaking codes and spying are only pieces of the intelligence puzzle. Without analysis, coordination, and decisions by policy-makers, intelligence is worthless, as in the case of the Pearl Harbor attack.

Pearl Harbor

The combination of collecting intelligence and reporting appropriate decisions was not working for the United States on December 7, 1941. The Japanese destroyed the American Pacific fleet, followed up with other crushing blows in the Pacific, and caused panic in California and elsewhere. Without doubt, an established central intelligence agency responsible for all information gathering could have avoided such a catastrophe. At the time most intelligence was uncoordinated. The United States had broken the Japanese code, but delays in reporting and a lack of coordination, resulted in a failure to inform American leaders.

The concept of a central intelligence agency started before America's entry into the war, in the early days of the European war when German troops *blitzkrieged* their way across France and threatened to defeat England.

A few people were involved and concerned. A British defeat would mean that Germany and its Axis

The Signal Intelligence Service (SIS) was established by the army in 1929 to control all army cryptologic activity. Under the leadership of William Friedman this small group (above) broke the Japanese diplomatic machine cipher. They did it without any access to the workings of the real Japanese machine.

This photo of Pearl Harbor was taken by a Japanese pilot shortly before the attack. Japanese intelligence, using spies in Hawaii, constructed in Japan huge scale models of the islands, harbors, ships, and bases and used these to train their pilots.

partners—Italy and Japan—would begin eyeing America. American interests were not really threatened by Mussolini's forays into Abyssinia or Hitler's demonic posturing. They threatened Europe more than America. However, if these dictators expanded the war, and if England were defeated, America would stand alone. America also had possessions in the Pacific and in Asia that the Japanese threatened. A breakdown in relations between Japan and America and Japan's need for raw materials and markets also caused concern. Few people recognized this in the late 1930s. President Franklin Roosevelt was worried about the Japanese and the situation in Germany and Italy. The British Secret Service was interested in developing ties with Americans sympathetic to her plight. In addition, one individual appeared on the scene who was concerned about the war and who saw firsthand the need for America to collect intelligence; this was William J. Donovan.

Some historians state that *after* Pearl Harbor the need for a central intelligence organization came into sharp public focus. Actually it began before that. It began in the early days of the war in Europe between England and Germany. Although President Roosevelt was interested in forming such a service, he could not do so because the United States was not at war. Also, there were political considerations. Some politicians wanted the United States to stay out of the war even if England was defeated. Setting up an intelligence agency would have added fuel to the fire that Roosevelt wanted war and was pro-British. Moreover, the FBI was involved in limited intelligence gathering in Latin America during the 1930s. J. Edgar Hoover was no man to cross and wanted all intelligence gathering, if any, to be done by the Federal Bureau of Investigation. The army and navy also held their domains to be sacred, as did the State Department, the War Department, and the Treasury.

Thus, Roosevelt had to contend with the antiwar politicians and the bureaucratic chiefs in his own

J. Edgar Hoover accepts appointment as honorary chief of the Cuban National Police. Ambassador Guillermo Belt of Cuba (left) presents the award. Before and during World War II, Hoover ran secret operations, training, and espionage all through Latin America. He strongly resented any interference in this area and was said to burn all Latin American files rather than help OSS during World War II or the CIA after the war. Hoover had FBI agents performing intelligence operations in Latin America for more than twenty years.

The photo above shows William Donovan in 1940 embarking on one of several secret trips for President Roosevelt. These trips eventually helped Donovan create the rationale, basis, and formula for the Office of Strategic Services and the forerunner for the establishment of the Central Intelligence Agency.

Above is Sir William Stephenson, known as "little Bill" and code-named Intrepid by an enterprising author. Stephenson, a Canadian businessman, helped set up secret British intelligence in New York City before America's entry in World War II. Many believe he was instrumental in convincing America's leaders to establish a central intelligence group. Many CIA personnel think most of the "Intrepid" story is pure fabrication.

administration. The American public was just not ready for a "spy" department. Americans also had long cherished their liberties and were not about to have an agency of the American government that might spy on its own citizens. It was alright for J. Edgar Hoover and his G-men to arrest gangsters and foreign agents, but not to have an agency that would function abroad or in the U.S. Each government department gathered its own intelligence, but there was little coordination and, as a result, that crucial phase of intelligence—*the analysis to prepare for decisions*—was neglected.

The efforts of William J. Donovan were effective in convincing President Roosevelt and the bureaucracies of various intelligence agencies to agree to one central agency. These efforts started at least two years before Pearl Harbor. They involved William J. Donovan exclusively and later, to some extent, the British Secret Service agent "Intrepid" and finally President Roosevelt.

Nathan Hale speaks the famous words just before he was executed by the English: "I only regret that I have but one life to lose for my country." A number of CIA agents have lost their lives for their country. Because of the need for secrecy, most have remained anonymous. Only recently have a few of the names and their missions become known.

The First American Spies:
Nathan Hale and Benjamin Tallmadge

Nathan Hale, arrested and condemned to death as a self-confessed American spy, was executed by the British in New York. General Howe, fearing an attack on the city, gave the order to William Cunningham, his brutal provost marshal. Eyewitnesses said Hale spoke the following words: "I only regret that I have but one life to lose for my Country." A British captain reported Hale "was calm, and bore himself with gentle dignity."

Nathan Hale, a Connecticut native and Yale graduate, volunteered to serve as a spy on an intelligence mission for General Washington. A scholar, athlete, and patriot, Hale took his Yale diploma to New York to pose as a schoolmaster. Probably betrayed by a Tory relative, he was arrested by the British. He was 21.

Although Hale is regarded as America's first spy hero, a classmate of Hale, Major Benjamin Tallmadge, was a truly successful spy. Tallmadge organized a ring that even today seems sophisticated. The patriot spies used aliases, codes, invisible ink, and even messages signaled by petticoats on clotheslines.

"Wild

Donovan's favorite photo of himself. It was taken shortly after his epic action at the Ourcq River. Most of his battalion was wiped out, and he was badly wounded. One story told by some former OSS officers claims that as Donovan was being taken out on a stretcher, Douglas MacArthur, commander of the section, wanted an explanation of the heavy casualties. Donovan complained (correctly) that there had been no artillery support. MacArthur, furious, tracked down the area artillery commander, Captain Harry S Truman, and "chewed him out." Truman never forgot this incident.

"Bill" Donovan

Donovan in his favorite OSS photo. Donovan inspired his men with encouragement and a typical American approach to problem-solving — "get things done and fast."

"Wild

William Donovan in his OSS uniform. This portrait hangs in CIA headquarters, Langley, Virginia.

Donovan's law offices in Rockefeller plaza. His firm maintains his awards, medals, and a portrait similar to the one at CIA.

Bill" Donovan

"Wild Bill" Donovan

William Joseph Donovan was born on January 1, 1883, in Buffalo, New York. Donovan's grandparents came from County Cork in Ireland. Donovan graduated from Columbia College and Law School and began to practice law in Buffalo. While practicing law, Donovan joined the New York National Guard and soon became a captain. Early in 1916, before America became involved in World War I, he crisscrossed Europe reporting on American relief efforts. In 1981, the CIA revealed that at that time, Donovan "probably" received "military intelligence" training from the British. The summer of 1916, however, saw his national guard unit mobilized for duty on the Mexican border against bandit-rebel Pancho Villa,

and he returned home to join it. Then the United States entered the war.

Donovan eventually was given command of New York's "Fighting 69th" regiment. The Fighting 69th, part of the Rainbow Division, fought in a number of battles and received heavy casualties. Donovan himself was wounded, and won the Distinguished Service Cross, Purple Heart, and the nation's highest medal, the Medal of Honor. He returned home a hero.

After the war Donovan resumed the practice of law, became involved in politics, and became a Justice Department lawyer arguing and winning cases before the Supreme Court. In 1932 he ran unsuccessfully as the Republican candidate for governor of New York.

Pancho Villa, Mexican guerrilla, proved an elusive quarry when Donovan was serving on the Mexican border.

With the war over Col. Donovan was a hero and made commander of the 165th infantry. Here he stands with Father Duffy, his mentor and confidant. They are shown in Remagen, Germany.

Donovan at the Supreme Court. Donovan won five major cases before the
Supreme Court.

Donovan received scores of medals and awards. He is the only intelligence officer to have received the Medal of Honor—it was awarded before he became involved in intelligence operations.

The photo at right shows Sir Stewart Menzies, wartime head of British Intelligence and a friend of Donovan. Menzies believed that the mantle of intelligence activities had to include the Americans. He also believed that only America with its vast economic and technological resources could foil Soviet subversion in the postwar world.

James R. Withrow, a partner in the law firm of Donovan, Leisure, Newton and Irvine, knew William Donovan for more than 20 years. Mr. Withrow was hired by General Donovan in the 1930s. He later served with him in OSS in the Pacific and Asian theatre during World War II.

Q *What was "Wild Bill" like?*

A The General was a wonderful man who's door was always open to everyone. Always friendly and positive.

Q *When did you start working for him?*

A I was just a junior lawyer then and the General had just returned from one of his many overseas trips. He had taken a top secret request from the British to Frank Knox. Knox passed the request on to the President.

Q *Was this the destroyer deal?*

A Yes. The Attorney General ruled that we couldn't do a deal with the British. They needed destroyers badly and the General and the President wanted it to go through. Roosevelt felt his hands were tied but he had to go along with what the Attorney General ruled. The General wouldn't take that so lightly so he called me into his offices and told me to go to work on it.

Q *What happened?*

A Well, I went to Washington and did some research. Quite a lot, and found legal precedent for helping a foreign power. After I did my research and prepared the legal work the General brought it up again and it was approved by the President and the Attorney General. The British got the destroyers (50, I believe) and we got lease rights to their bases for 99 years.

Q *A pretty good deal for the United States.*

A Well, yes, we still have the bases. The destroyers we gave them were not very good but they used them for convoy patrol. The real significance was that the U.S. stepped over the neutrality line and overtly aided the British. It was a big morale lifter for the British and cemented Donovan's relationship to British intelligence and its government's policy.

Q *Today, historians believe that this destroyer deal was the first step in setting up an American central intelligence agency. How do you feel?*

A That's probably right because both the General and Sir William Stephenson were advocating this.

Q *Was Donovan co-opted by the British?*

A Not at all. That's nonsense. Some British writers would like you to believe it. You see, the General traveled overseas constantly and he was worried about the United States not being prepared for war. Most of his trips were at his own expense and he remembered the terrible carnage in World War I. I am sure he admired the British set-up, but no one could co-opt the General or control him.

This photo shows Donovan in 1948 in Berlin.

Donovan shown here leaving the White House just before Pearl Harbor.

To his Fighting 69th colleagues he was "Wild Bill" to his OSS men he was "the General". Roosevelt loved to call him "Wild Bill" in a loud and joking manner.

In April 1941 Donovan sent to his close friend Secretary of the Navy Frank Knox a report on setting up a new U.S. central intelligence agency. In it he stated his ideas regarding such an organization: "Intelligence operations should not be controlled by party exigencies. It is one of the most vital means of national defense. As such it should be headed by some one appointed by the President directly responsible to him and to no one else. It should have a fund solely for the purpose of foreign investigation and the expenditures under this fund should be secret and made solely at the discretion of the President."

Donovan thought the service should not usurp the home duties performed by the FBI and the military intelligence organizations. Rather, it should "(1) have sole charge of intelligence work abroad, (2) coordinate the activities of military and naval attachés and

General Donovan, Director of the Office of Strategic Services. Donovan continued to travel all over the world and made numerous trips to Europe during the war. His colleagues describe his energy and activities as almost superhuman. Always positive and friendly, this personable Irish-American was able to instill in his agents esprit de corps and loyalty.

others in the collection of information abroad, (3) classify and interpret all information from whatever source obtained to be available for the President and for such of the services as he would designate." To ensure the full cooperation of all the departments Donovan suggested that the President appoint an advisory committee "consisting at least of the Assistant Secretaries of State, Treasury, War, Navy and Justice...."

Donovan believed, like Churchill, that "modern war operates on more fronts than battle fronts" and that "each combatant seeks to dominate the whole field of communications." Consequently, no defense system would be effective unless it recognized and dealt with this fact.

Donovan, before the war was a successful lawyer before the Supreme Court.

59

America's first civilian spy headquarters. It served as home of OSS with its odd assortment of scholars, writers and lawyers. 25th and E Streets, Washington, D.C.

William Stephenson named Donovan Q. After the war Stephenson claimed this was his only code name. Actually he used many during the war.

FDR also knew his choice to head the new organization would be an important factor in getting the agency started. Besides Donovan, he considered his socialite friend and sailing partner Vincent Astor, and he thought of Fiorello La Guardia, then mayor of New York. Hoover and businessman Nelson Rockefeller were also possibilities.

By the end of May 1941, Donovan completed his paper, entitled "Memorandum of Establishment of Service of Strategic Information," and submitted it to FDR. On June 18, Donovan was summoned to the White House to discuss what he had written. That same day, the President approved the plan and ordered the formation of what initially was called the Office of the Coordinator of Information (COI).

ERNSTEIN-BIRNBACK

NEW YORK
Herald Tribune
LATE CITY EDITION

THE WEATHER
Today: Occasional rain, cloudy in afternoon, little change in temperature
Tomorrow: Partly cloudy and continued cold
Temperature Yesterday: Max. 47 Min. 40
Detailed Report on Page 9, Sec. III

Vol. C No. 34,475

Copyright, 1941,
New York Tribune, Inc.

SUNDAY, APRIL 6, 1941

Section One

TEN CENTS
New York City and V...

Germans March on Yugoslavia and Greece
Two Nations Defiant as Balkan War Begins
Moscow and Belgrade Sign Friendship Pac[t]

Roosevelt Acts To Bar Strike At U. S. Steel

Calls Murray to Capital as C. I. O. Orders Men Out Tuesday Midnight

Mediator Assigned By Miss Perkins

Union Asks $52,000,000 Rise and Closed Shop; 261,000 Are Affected

By The United Press
PITTSBURGH, April 5—President Roosevelt personally has intervened in the threatened work stoppage of the mills of the United States Steel Corporation and has summoned Philip Murray, C. I. O. president, to Washington for a conference. It was learned tonight.

It was learned authoritatively that the President had summoned Mr. Murray because he feared a strike in United States Steel mills would threaten the success of the nation's defense program.

Peace in Ford Strike Tomorrow Or Tuesday Seen by Conciliator

By Geoffrey Parsons Jr.
A Staff Correspondent
DETROIT, April 5—The strike that has kept 85,000 men idle at the River Rouge plant of the Ford Motor Company since last Wednesday may be settled Monday or Tuesday, Governor Murray D. Van Wagoner of Michigan and Federal Conciliator James F. Dewey announced here tonight.

After a day of conferences, alternately with officials of the company and representatives of the United Automobile Workers, an affiliate of the Congress of Industrial Organizations, the Governor and the conciliator issued a statement which pro-
(Continued on page 32, column 2)

200,000 See Army Day Parade, With New Guns, Draftees, Rain

'They've Got Everything,' Sodden Spectator Says as Mechanized Might Rolls Down Fifth Ave.; Downpour Thins Ranks of 2½-Hour March

The thirteenth annual Army Day parade, the mightiest military display the city has seen since the World War, which the United States entered twenty-four years ago today, moved down upper Fifth Avenue yesterday afternoon. It was cheered by some 200,000 citizens, who with Governor Herbert H. Lehman, Mayor

Coal Settlement

Assault Finds Yugoslavs Set To Resist Foe

Borders Closed a Day in Advance, Ships Called Back, Planes on Watch

Cabinet Is Ready To Flee Belgrade

American Envoy Plans to Stay; Few U. S. Citizens Remain, British Depart

By Russell Hill
By Telephone to the Herald Tribune
Copyright, 1941, New York Tribune, Inc.
BELGRADE, April 5—With the zero hour at hand, Yugoslavia waited calmly tonight for the German army to move. Military preparations were being completed. Diplomatic activity had virtually ceased.

Yugoslavia is assuming more and more the aspect of an armed camp. All frontiers, with the exception of the Greek one, were closed today. Private cars have requisitioned and a censorship over mail has been imposed.

British Block

Hitler Te[lls] Balkan Ar[my] Hour Is Co[me]

Berlin Radio Announces Troops Have Cr[ossed] Border in New [Blitz]

Fuehrer Puts Bl[ame] On British Intr[igue]

Calls U. S. a Provocation; Promises Salonica Will Be Another Dunk[irk]

By The Associated Press
BERLIN, April 5 (Sunday)—German radio broadcast early an order by Fuehrer Adolf Hitler to the German army to march into Yugoslavia and Greece.

Dr. Paul Joseph Goebbels, Propaganda Minister, who begun to march, said the move was not an attack upon the "Greek people," but was directed solely at the policy of striking Great Britain wherever its forces appear. He also accused Yugoslavia of a similar to the interest of that country

Soviet Neutrality Pledge

NEW THEATER OF WAR IN BALKANS—Area where Germany is at war with Yugoslavia and Greece

Herald Tribune map—Rickert

This newspaper headline came out right after German intelligence agents reported Donovan trying to "inflame the Balkans". Donovan in his travels to that part of the world actually tried to stop the Germans from obtaining any more allies. Donovan had already been making contacts for espionage operations in Yugoslavia and other Balkan countries two years before America became involved.

Nelson Rockefeller (left, here with his brother Laurance), president of New York's Rockefeller Center, where Donovan, Sir William Stephenson, and Japanese intelligence agents were located. Rockefeller ran his own secret operations in Latin America as a private businessman, and he also served as FDR's Coordinator of Inter-American Affairs. Consequently, he did not want Donovan interfering with his intelligence activities south of the border.

Two candidates to head America's spy agency. Eleanor Roosevelt felt New York Mayor Fiorello La Guardia (right) would be a good choice. FBI Director J. Edgar Hoover, who ran a Secret Intelligence Service in South America, thought he was the best candidate; he jealously watched Donovan's OSS throughout World War II.

The news of COI, which was formally established on July 11, was greeted enthusiastically by the British, who had pushed for intelligence collaboration between the United States and Britain. In New York, Donovan's close friend William Stephenson (later Sir William, and known today as "Intrepid") cabled Menzies in London: "You can imagine how relieved I am after three months of battle and jockeying for position in Washington that our man is in a position of such importance to our efforts."

Not unexpectedly, the news was less welcome in Berlin. Shortly after Pearl Harbor and America's entry into the war, the German propaganda machine generated the following report: "Behind the scenes in Washington, a secret bureau has been created, a bureau to which very few have entrée. This new office is under the personal leadership of Colonel Donovan.

Vincent Astor (left), yachtsman and world traveler, served as a one-man, unofficial intelligence unit for his friend and sailing partner Franklin Roosevelt.

Donovan, now a General, as head of OSS. Here he is seen leaving the White House. Donovan made scores of trips to the White House during the war. They are some of the only pictures taken of him during the war.

Donovan made a number of trips to Europe during the 1930s and early 1940s for his legal business and his (and FDR's) "information" interests. Listed below are the itineraries for two major trips, the first a combination of several personal visits in the spring and summer of 1939, and the second a trip made in 1941 at FDR's request.

TRIP ONE — A Personal Visit

Country	Visited
Spain	Franco's troops at the Ebro River battle (Donovan escaped a hand grenade thrown at him)
Germany	German Army maneuvers near Nuremberg
France, Belgium, Luxembourg, the Netherlands, Scandinavia	Heads of government, military leaders
Libya	Military emplacements
United Kingdom	Churchill, Chamberlain, Stewart Menzies
Germany	Admiral Canaris

TRIP TWO — At FDR's Request

Great Britain, Gibraltar, Malta, Cairo, Athens, Belgrade, Sofia, Athens, Albania, Turkey, Cyprus, Palestine, Cairo, Baghdad, Cairo, Malta, Gibraltar, Madrid, Lisbon, London, Dublin.

Donovan in 1952 broadcasting an address to veterans of the Fighting 69th. On February 22 — Washington's Birthday — the Fighting Irish under Donovan were the first to go into the front lines to hold a divisional sector. Donovan told the veterans "that World War I was a tough fight, but we have a tougher one ahead." He meant the Soviet threat.

"Colonel Donovan's office . . . has grown into the largest espionage and sabotage bureau that has so far been seen in any Anglo-Saxon country. It is, confessedly, the aim of Donovan to create for Roosevelt a huge fifth column in Europe and South America. Terroristic attempts, acts of sabotage, revolts, corruption, bribery . . . are the main points of the Roosevelt-Donovan program. . . ."

"'Wild Bill,' as he is known in America, first came to our attention when Roosevelt sent him as special envoy . . . to the South of Europe, in order to incite the people of those countries to rebellion against Germany. The role Colonel Donovan played in Belgrade is still fresh in our minds, and he can be blamed for the tragic Serbian affair. . . .

"A second and *more monstrous meddling* is at present under way, and as usual under the leadership of Colonel Donovan. Roosevelt has named the Colonel Coordinator of Information. Hiding behind this title he is brewing a Jewish-Democratic crisis which is directed at all of Europe. Donovan has unlimited power. He can spend any sum of money he desires. He can have as many assistants as he chooses. And he can get any information he desires.

Roosevelt's belief in COI was confirmed by the Pearl Harbor disaster, which could possibly have been averted had there been a coordinated intelli-

gence effort. At 2:00 A.M. on December 8, over sandwiches at the end of a long day of conferences at the White House, Roosevelt, knowing how important coordinated intelligence would be during the coming war, told Donovan: "It's a good thing you got me started on this."

After World War II Donovan became assistant prosecutor at the Nuremberg war crimes trials, but left before the trials began. He then returned to his law practice. He also served as a government consultant. On July 29, 1953, President Eisenhower appointed him ambassador to Thailand, and he served in this position until he resigned in September 1954, returning once again to law and consulting. He died on February 8, 1959, and is buried in Arlington National Cemetery.

Donovan hoped he would be named head of the CIA after the war. When he was not he nevertheless continued to serve his country. In 1953 he was appointed ambassador to Thailand. He is shown here with (from left to right) his aide Lieutenant William vanden Heuvel, his daughter-in-law Mary Grandin Donovan, and his granddaughter Patricia as he returned to Bangkok after meeting with President Eisenhower.

Donovan was legal advisor to many prominent Americans and companies, including Claire Chennault's Civil Air Transport. This photo was taken in 1950 when he visited Chennault (left) at his offices in Hong Kong. In the middle is Colonel Roy Heston, U.S. Air Liaison Officer.

Fritz Kuhn   **Father Charles E. Coughlin**   **Sen. Gerald P. Nye**

The isolationist group embraced very different people — Charles Lindbergh was one who admired the technological efficiencies of the Third Reich, and Father Couglin and Fritz Kuhn and his nazi-aping German American Bund. In addition Roosevelt faced pressures in Congress and his own administration against helping the allies. Ambassador Joseph Kennedy was adamant about not giving aid to England. Donovan's travels convinced Roosevelt to set up an intelligence group and to overtly aid Britain.

John L. Lewis   **Colonel Charles A. Lindbergh**   **Norman Thomas**

Donovan was one of the few who recognized the need for an intelligence agency and the need to help Britain. During 1940 to 1941 the "Great Debate" took place. The debate went on in Congress, at public rallies, the radio, at universities — where ever people gathered. The leading isolationist group was the America First Committee. It was anti-Semitic and anti-England. There were also fascist and communist groups opposed to the war.

Donovan's Legacy

An Intelligence Dynasty

Donovan knew how to recruit, train, and inspire. The Donovan influence helped direct the four men below to the position of Director of Central Intelligence. These four DCIs have demonstrated that America was equal to the new game of spying. All four are regarded as the best directors the agency has had. Moreover, each has followed the basic philosophy established by Donovan for America's intelligence service—good intelligence gathering and clandestine activities.

Allen Welsh Dulles is regarded as one of the most successful spymasters. His leadership was crucial in the early stages of the Central Intelligence Agency. Dulles, former head of OSS in Switzerland, continued Donovan's guidelines for gathering intelligence and covert operations.

Richard Helms served with Donovan during OSS days. He was appointed Director of Central Intelligence by President Johnson. Under Helms, the CIA's budget quadrupled compared to the agency's founding in 1947. Helms is credited with the professional expansion of clandestine operations.

William E. Colby, served heroically for Donovan behind enemy lines in Norway and in France. Colby served as Director of the CIA during the Nixon and Ford administrations. Colby also worked as an attorney for Donovan's law firm in New York.

William J. Casey was chief of Secret Intelligence in London for Donovan and successfully organized many agents and covert operations into Germany and France. President Reagan appointed Casey as Director of Central Intelligence. Casey has to be given credit as the man who brought the CIA back to full strength.

The

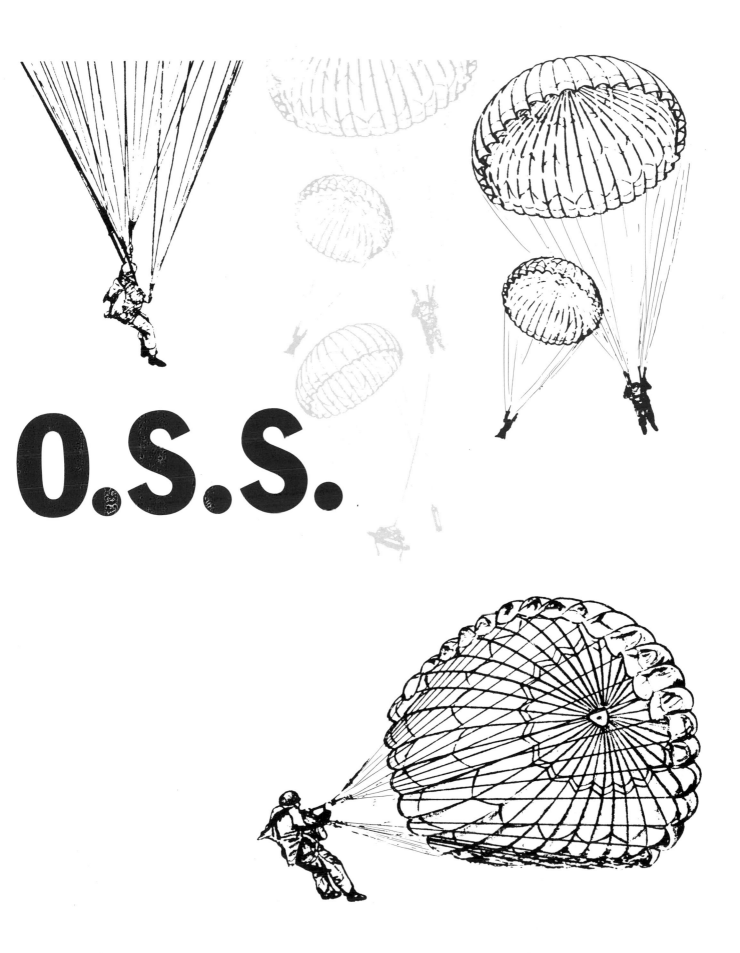

O.S.S.

The

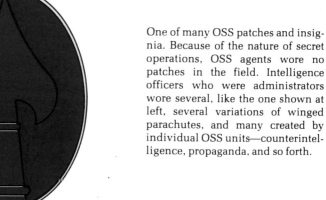

One of many OSS patches and insignia. Because of the nature of secret operations, OSS agents wore no patches in the field. Intelligence officers who were administrators wore several, like the one shown at left, several variations of winged parachutes, and many created by individual OSS units—counterintelligence, propaganda, and so forth.

OSS headquarters at 2430 E Street, NW, Washington, DC. It was the first building to house a centralized intelligence operation.

Beginnings

President Roosevelt first introduced an intelligence service to America in 1941. Originally known as the Office of the Coordinator of Information, it was renamed the Office of Strategic Services (OSS) a year later.

Head of the service was 57-year-old William J. Donovan, already a hero from World War I. He was also a millionaire, the head of a successful Wall Street law firm, and a man of vigorous and adventurous resourcefulness.

His original brief was to collect and analyze information for the President about international events which posed a potential threat to the safety of the country.

At the time of Pearl Harbor, the service was newly formed and in no position of strength. Although a complicated cipher used by the Japanese was unraveled, the data assembled from their messages was never analyzed. Had it been, it would have revealed clear evidence that the Japanese were targeting Pearl Harbor for immediate attack.

Donovan's ebullient charm and dedicated beliefs in the service fired the enthusiasm of many idiosyncratic personalities. He was able to recruit some of the most brilliant and colorful figures in the country into his organization. They included bankers, lawyers, industrialists, poets, academics, playwrights, and filmmakers. Among them were such names as James Roosevelt (one of FDR's sons), diplomat John Wiley, scholar and poet Archibald MacLeish, playwright

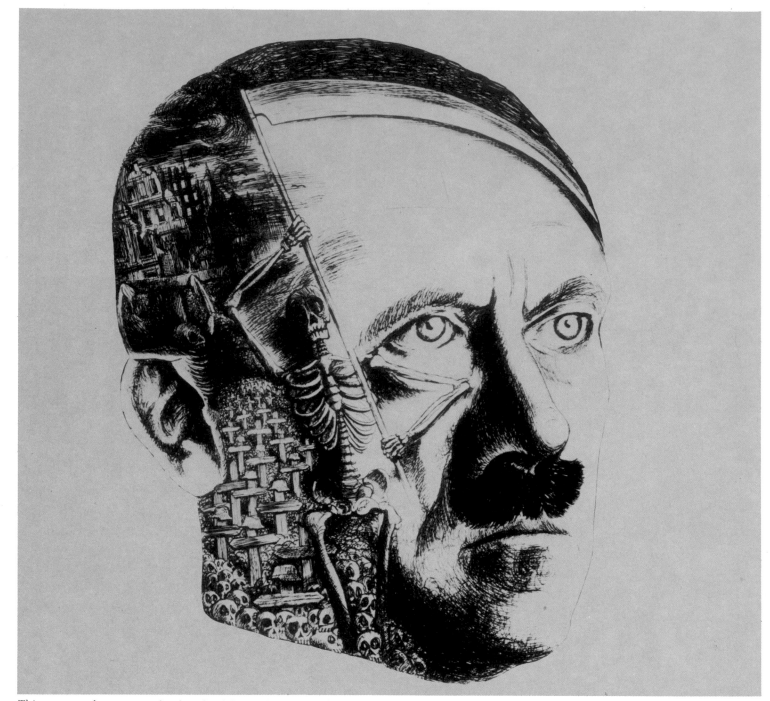

This propaganda poster was developed and dropped over Germany and occupied territories. OSS artists devised this and other more innovative ones. A small series of comic books was developed and designed to fit in a German soldier's tunic. The comic books usually contained obscene stories about Hitler, Goering, and other Nazi leaders. If the soldiers were found with them, they would be disciplined, causing morale problems (or at least this was OSS's intent). OSS also forged documents and operated its own newspaper, printing, and publishing enterprises.

Robert Sherwood, Arthur Schlesinger, Jr., Allen Dulles, and filmmaker John Ford.

OSS Organization

The concept of an American intelligence service was strenuously encouraged by Winston Churchill and the British government. They were eager to pool their resources with official allies, but they looked for assurances that sensitive intelligence would be carefully handled without risk to vital sources of information. That called for trained, highly skilled operators.

William Donovan observed the British methods at work, and later fashioned OSS in a similar mold. He quickly realized the importance of counter-espionage, the control of German espionage by which false information was fed to the enemy, and cryptanalysis, which penetrated enemy intelligence. Both methods were successfully used in OSS.

OSS used covert and overt operations. They trained paramilitary action teams who landed behind enemy

This photo shows OSS handiwork. This train was blown up by a Jed team in France on the eve of D-Day. More than 7,000 photos like this and more than 250 films were recently released to the National Archives by the CIA.

President Roosevelt instructed General Eisenhower to fully cooperate with OSS operations. In the beginning Eisenhower was reluctant, but as OSS operations expanded and succeeded, Eisenhower became convinced of the necessity of covert operations both during and after wartime.

lines to conduct sabotage, support guerrilla forces and send back important military data.

It was originally estimated that a team of 92 people could fulfill the obligations of the organization. From its meager beginnings—the service was allocated two and a half offices in Washington—it mushroomed to become a clandestine empire of about 16,000 in number, including staffs at home and overseas. At home, they worked in a complex of buildings all represented by the single address: 2430 E St., NW, Washington, DC.

OSS was financed largely by secret funds and Donovan's expenditures were given minimal official scrutiny. When he requested a working budget of $10

OSS
Form 69 (Revised)

OFFICE OF STRATEGIC SERVICES

OFFICIAL DISPATCH

DATE September 23, 1944

FROM

USTRAVIC, LONDON

	PRIORITY
	ROUTINE
	DEFERRED

TO

OFFICE OF STRATEGIC SERVICES

DISTRIBUTION

IN 20897

(FOR ACTION)	(FOR INFORMATION)
Og 15,346 DIRECTOR	SECRETARIAT, BIGELOW, MEDTO, ETO, MAGRUDER, SI, X-2, OG

U. S. GOVERNMENT PRINTING OFFICE   16—37883-1

RECEIVED IN CODE OR CIPHER   SECRET

#77384. From Livermore to Donovan.

I have received your letter concerning proposed use of OG's. Have talked to our people in Paris and here. Yesterday I discussed plan with Brigadier Maunsell of SHAEF. He stated that a regiment is to be formed which will have several companies. In this will be British SAS and SOE and some American Rangers and OSS is asked to put in some personnel. On this basis we would have little control of our men. The function of this regiment would be to arrest and seize every individuals or underground groups behind our lines in Germany. After careful consideration I recommend that OG's do not participate in the proposed regiment for the following reasons.

(1) Our men are Infantry who are specially trained parachutists. The men wish to and have a right to retain their status as parachutists. In such a regiment they would lose their parachute status and pay.

(2) The men and officers wish to continue fighting the German army or Japanese army and do not wish to do semi-police work. If no further operations against Germans seem possible they would like to go to Far East either as now constituted or else be transferred to parachute units of the Army.

(3) The proposed regiment would be British controlled and we would only be contributing personnel which is an unsatisfactory basis.

In view of the above I make the following recommendations:

(1) That the Norwegian OG remain temporarily in UK pending possible operations

This recently released memo to Donovan discusses an administrative complaint Donovan had to answer. The British needed men and requested OSS personnel. The memo shows the esprit de corps of OSS and the fact that the OSS group discussed preferred to remain parachutists and agents in a combat role. Donovan turned the British request down, but still sent agents of his own to arrest and handle German individuals. Some of these agents and Germans worked for CIA after the war.

OSS
Form 69a

OFFICE OF STRATEGIC SERVICES

OFFICIAL DISPATCH

PAGE____

FROM

TO OFFICE OF STRATEGIC SERVICES

REF. NO.

London

RECEIVED

16—31461a-1   U. S. GOVERNMENT PRINTING OFFICE

SECRET

(2)   That the one German group be held in Italy and that it be augmented by other German speakers to a force of not over 100 and it be held as a reserve pending developments in Germany which may be used for OSS purposes as required.

(3)   That all other OG's be returned form ETO and MEDTO to Washington as speedily as possible as they are withdrawn from operations. Speed is essential to get our men moving before shipping to us gets congested and also so that the men may be used elsewhere with the minimum delay.

(4)   That inquiry be made into the possibility of using these men as a parachute unit in Far East and if this is not possible that they be processed back to Army. Request you cable me your decision and send copy to Caserta.

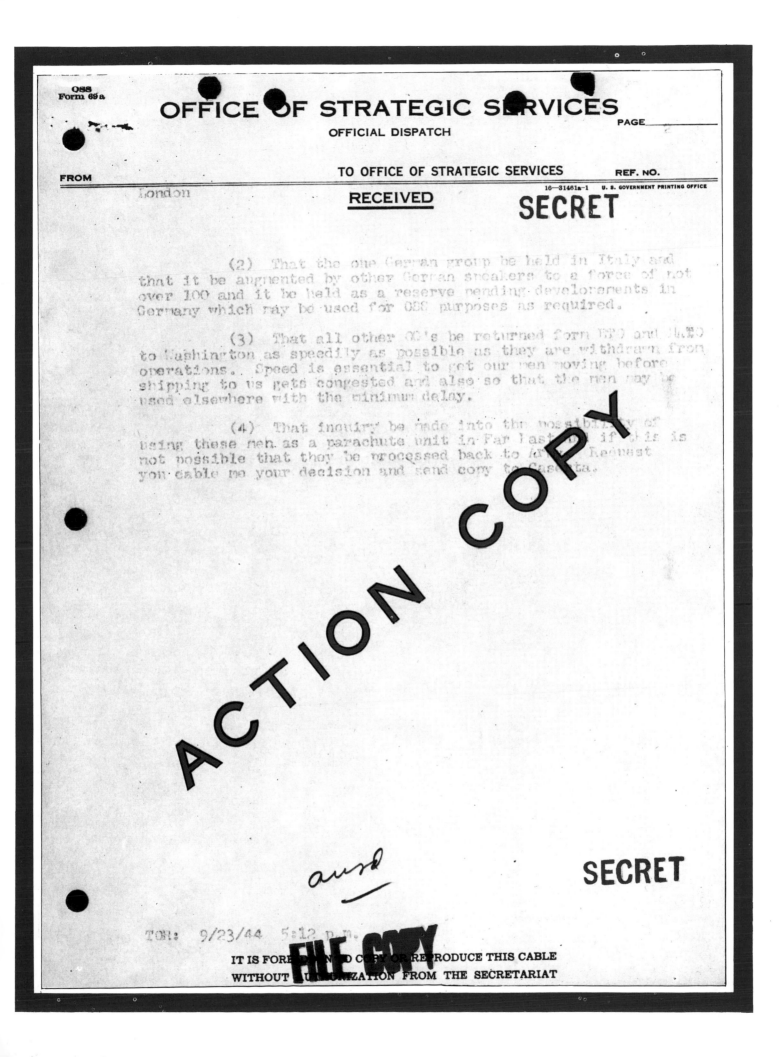

ausk

SECRET

TOR: 9/23/44 5:12 p.m.

Admiral Jean Darlan, French High Commissioner of North Africa, and General Eisenhower in North Africa. Shortly after this photo was taken Darlan was assassinated. For a number of years it was believed Darlan was killed for being sympathetic to the Germans. Recently released documents indicate OSS may have been involved as revenge because Darlan did not support U.S. landings in North Africa. Eisenhower felt Darlan's nonsupport resulted in thousands of unnecessary casualties. Darlan promised OSS that French troops would not impede the landings. Carleton Coon, Donovan's OSS man in North Africa, was apparently involved in the negotiations with Darlan and knew who assassinated him.

million, the money was forthcoming with the barest formalities. He merely put his signature to a certificate that the money had been spent in the national interest.

OSS became a major force in the events of World War II and was the basis of the CIA today.

Torch

It was clear that the occupation of North Africa would become a decisive factor in the outcome of the war. And in 1942 the search was on for a strong, charismatic French leader who could ignite a movement of revolt and weld together the Gaullists and other political factions against the Nazi dominated government.

Every aspect of intelligence operations became of vital importance to the North African landing known as Torch that took place on November 8, 1942. Landing beaches, terrain, and customs of the country were thoroughly researched, while undercover agents in neutral territory on unoccupied French soil became useful intermediaries in testing and shaping the political thinking of French armed forces. They stayed keenly attuned to current mood, and found strong support for the U.S. among the majority of the French army. Given an opportunity of liberating France it seemed they would choose to lean towards

A variety of OSS men. Otto Doering (top) was the behind-the-scenes manager of OSS, Donovan's law partner, and executive officer of OSS. Colonel David Bruce (middle) was chief of OSS in Europe. Henry B. Hyde (bottom) ran secret intelligence in Algiers, the main base of operations into France. Hyde later succeeded Allen Dulles as OSS intelligence chief in Switzerland. All OSS operatives used codenames so that if they were captured they could not reveal the names of their comrades. Captain Bazooka was typical of such codenames.

CAPT^N BAZOOKA

Americans, rather than the Germans.

This was the first important overseas operation of the OSS and William Donovan was fully aware of the hazardous and delicate nature of the assignment. The mission was a minefield of potential danger and Donovan illuminated the issues clearly in a list of warning imperatives.

It was vital, he noted, to avoid any action which would bring the French fleet into the war on the side of the enemy; nor could the Germans be permitted to occupy French North Africa without the French fleet and army being brought into action against them. It was of paramount importance not to provoke any substantial French action against American forces.

The Allies, it was commonly agreed, wanted to fight the Germans, not the French.

Using maximum diplomatic skill, the OSS's targeted objective was to ease the way for the fierce confrontation ahead by capitalizing on any clandestine contacts or resources that might ensure an unopposed landing.

From their vast underground net of operations there emerged the name of General Henri Giraud, professional army officer and devoted patriot who had escaped back to his French homeland after capture by the Germans.

The OSS obtained private letters and secret documentation indicating that the general had his heart set

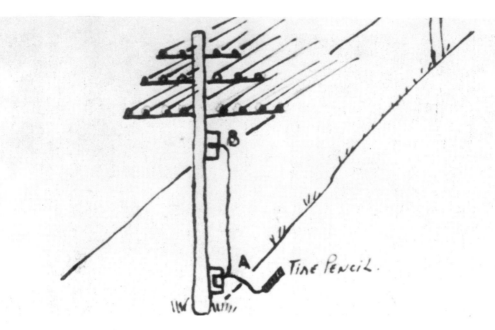

Secret, efficient, and quick were the watchwords when training an agent to blow up a telephone pole. OSS trained thousands of operatives in foreign occupied lands to sabotage railways, switching stations, and telegraph and communications lines. German reinforcements during the Normandy invasion were seriously delayed by OSS tactics.

These two OSS officers sport several OSS patches. The officer on the left has three and the officer on the right one. The more common were the ones on the left officer's hat and right pocket.

on a national insurrection against the Germans. All evidence recommended him as a natural leader and the OSS arranged a secret meeting between Giraud and representatives of the top U.S. military forces.

But in the final outcome the French general was able to join Allied forces in Gibraltar only a few hours before the landings. At that point Giraud became an embarrassment to General Eisenhower, when he demanded command of the invasion. French military honor, he argued, forbade his participation without top rank.

Later the OSS acted as joint intermediaries with American military forces in establishing an agreement with Vichy Admiral Jean Darlan who stopped the fighting in return for the post of high commissioner in North Africa. Giraud received the lesser post of commander of military forces.

OSS achievements in North Africa—although not a total success—secured a notable reputation for the service. They became recognized by the European Military Command as skilled operators in the areas of clandestine activities and paramilitary operations as well as diplomatic and political maneuvers.

D-Day

Late in the Spring of 1944—with the long-awaited invasion of France still ahead—the OSS dedicated its

President Truman talks with General Donovan and artist Henry L'Aussucq in 1945. L'Aussucq was instrumental in organizing underground operations in France in preparation for D-Day. He was a Pittsburgh artist who Donovan found had very good connections in France.

In preparation for D-Day, OSS had to establish its own engineering and mapmaking operation. Contrary to popular belief, France was not a well-mapped country. OSS mapped every inch of France and provided agents with detailed maps of cities, towns, and the countryside.

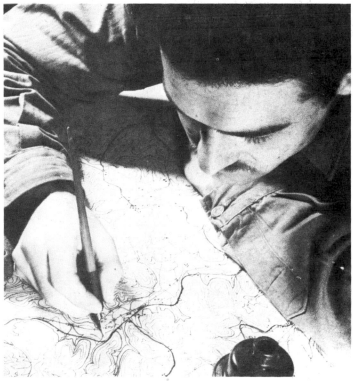

efforts to gathering every scrap of significant information that might contribute to Allied success.

Already its paramilitary operations in the Mediterranean had proved of strategic importance in deflecting some of Germany's military power away from France at this most critical time in Allied planning. The OSS thoroughly penetrated France with hundreds of agents engaged in clandestine operations. Some agents parachuted into occupied territory, others entered via the Pyrenees and landed under cover of darkness by submarine or fast PT boat. Once in France, they were smuggled to the safety of underground hideouts. A network of welcoming

The jumpmaster (standing at top) is William Colby, later Director of Central Intelligence. Colby operated in France and Norway for OSS. The photos at right show Colby (top) and the other members of Jedburgh Team Bruce in 1944: Lieutenant Jacques Favel (middle) and Sergeant Louis Giry (bottom), both Free French officers.

Colby and comrades pay final tribute to men lost when their Liberator crashed during Operation "Rype," Norway, April 1945.

homes throughout France brought them protective cover, and provided them with facilities for transmitting vital information on their special radio equipment.

They radioed news that the crack Panzer Lehr Division had been seen in France and was not on the Russian front as commonly believed. Forearmed, Eisenhower was able to pitch the full crushing force of a top American division against it.

OSS agents managed to seize the plans of two massive war production plants: an explosives factory and an oil refining factory, which became targets for attack by Allied planes. Both sites were demolished.

Skilled Jedburgh operators parachuted into France to arm, train, and mastermind the movements of the

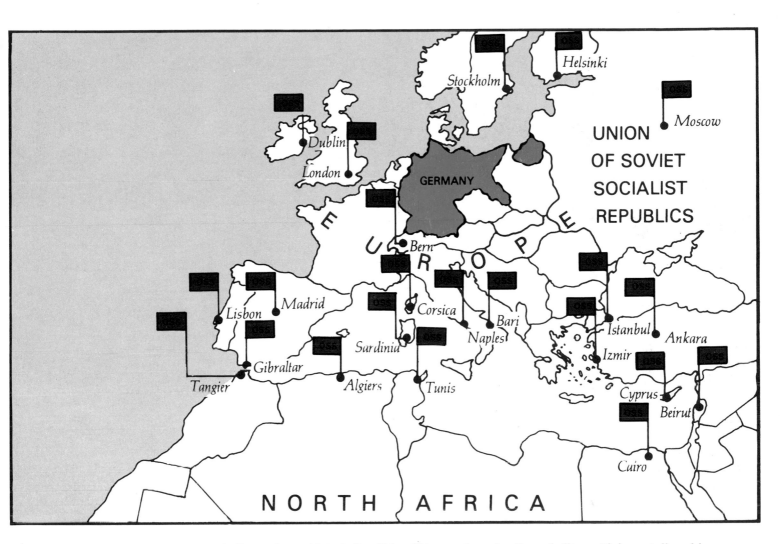

OSS had offices in the United States and all over the world, including China. This map shows locations of offices with large staffs, safehouses, clandestine training bases, radio stations, and other headquarters for signal intercept and covert operations in the European theatre. During the war some espionage was carried out against the Soviets, but it was not successful because of Soviet countermeasures.

French Resistance. Each team of "Jeds" was a group of three Allied officers and a radio operator who worked with large numbers of Resistance fighters. Already 50,000 Frenchmen belonged to the Maquis and their numbers swelled daily.

The job of the Jedburghs was to equip the Resistance with thorough training in espionage, explosives, medical care, and handling a rifle. In intensified air drops, thousands of tons of weapons and ammunition were parachuted into the country by the British and Americans.

The "Jeds" ultimate objective, by means of wireless contact with London, was to bring the entire movement under the order of the supreme Allied commander, General Eisenhower.

In the last weeks before the invasion, OSS Chief William J. Donovan filed a top secret report containing dramatic intelligence received from Allen Dulles, the agency's representative in Switzerland. A group of German emissaries, among them high ranking military figures, proposed an overthrow of Hitler and the Nazi regime. The conspirators made an approach to the OSS, making a declaration of intentions to be carried out provided they received an assurance of direct negotiation with Western powers thereafter.

For the Allies, the information brought a heartening insight into the prevalent fears of the enemy. Never-

The lamb is ready for slaughter.

The roses are not blooming.

Mr. Clark has arrived home.

The grey fox has taken the bait.

Mrs. Sinclair has gone to the opera.

The wine is red.

Bletchley Park, headquarters of secret British intelligence operations involving Ultra. The Ultra secret was not revealed until 30 years after the war ended. The Ultra material—the deciphered messages of the German military command—provided OSS will valuable information necessary to covert operations. OSS also ran its own signals intercept operation and had its own tailor shop and radio bases.

Inset: Each evening the BBC broadcast personal messages like these. In reality, these messages were coded instructions for agents operating behind enemy lines.

theless the Allied course was clear. The war would be ended solely by military means.

With increased confidence in the undertaking ahead, Eisenhower issued a signal from his English battle headquarters in Portsmouth: hornpipe plus six. D-Day would be June 6, 1944.

Nightly after the 9 o'clock news, BBC Radio from London broadcast a program of "personal messages." Coded, intelligible only to agents receiving them on French soil, they contained orders of secret missions to be undertaken.

On the eve of the invasion, the program extended far beyond its normal length. Because isolated instances of sabotage could lead the Germans to suspect the time and place of invasion, the Resistance was commanded to follow a total course of action throughout the entire country. "The wine is red" was the coded message that triggered a violent wave of action from the Resistance everywhere in France.

It attacked German headquarters, ambushed messengers, cut telephone and telegraph wires, and carried out other acts of sabotage that deprived the German High Command of intelligence, causing

The most frequent meeting places for OSS. Yale University served as a training facility in languages and tradecraft. Camp Ritchie, Maryland, trained thousands in covert operations. The 2430 building served as headquarters. The St. Regis Hotel served as a center for Donovan's clandestine meetings and interviews. Rockefeller Center served as William Stephenson's offices and a microwave transmission center. The White House served as a top level place where Donovan briefed President Roosevelt on OSS operations. After the war CIA kept its contacts with Yale, Stephenson, and used the 2430 building as well.

major chaos that supported the successful invasion landings made by the Allies.

It was their supreme task and a fitting tribute to the OSS.

Asia

Wartime leaders Franklin Roosevelt and Winston Churchill agreed to give OSS a most important role to play in the Burma campaign.

It led to some of the most successful, irregular military operations of the entire war.

OSS agents—just 20 strong when activities first started in 1942—penetrated the tribal area near the borders of Burma, China, and Thailand, and set out to organize Kachin mountain people into a unit of guerrilla fighters.

Former prison guard Colonel Carl Eifler (above) ran OSS's Detachment 101 in Asia. Detachment 101 was a guerrilla warfare experiment that achieved its greatest success against the Japanese during the Burma campaign.

This navy Seal, now used by CIA on covert operations, owes his existence and training to OSS. Groups of guerrillas and commandos trained by OSS operated throughout World War II by harassing the enemy.

The number of OSS agents drawn into the operation grew rapidly and eventually they became Detachment 101, led by Carl Eifler, a tough former prison guard. He served under the command of General Joseph ("Vinegar Joe") Stilwell as senior U.S. Army chief in India and Burma.

With only nominal resources, he was pitched against a Japanese army of resolute single mindedness and great military strength.

The OSS-led American Kachin Rangers held the key to Allied victory in Southeast Asia. In all, 10,000 tribesmen took part in sabotage action against the Japanese. They operated as much as 250 miles behind

General Douglas MacArthur (left) never fully succeeded in keeping OSS out of the Pacific. During this meeting in Hawaii with President Roosevelt and Admirals William Leahy and Chester Nimitz, two OSS agents are in the background.

Japanese lines and their successful operations and constant harassment led to a number of substantial victories, including the recapture of Myitkyina Airfield and the sinking of river vessels carrying fuel.

A new Anglo-American headquarters was created in South East Asia Command (SEAC) of which Admiral Louis Mountbatten, chief of the British commandos and a cousin of the king, was appointed supreme commander. General Stilwell was named deputy commander of SEAC.

OSS and British SOE (Special Operations Executive) forces worked together amicably in the formation of a new division (P division) under the command of a British officer and an OSS deputy to coordinate clandestine activities. The American service later strengthened its independence by creating a new unit inside OSS (Detachment 404) to organize all Southeast Asian operations.

Cooperation between OSS and SOE during this time resulted in a supreme example of Allied teamwork in clandestine services.

Donovan prepared a secret memorandum for President Roosevelt's eyes only. He stated his beliefs in the need of a permanent intelligence service. "When our enemies are defeated," he wrote in the fall of 1944, "the demand will be equally pressing for information that will aid us in solving the problems of peace."

He visualized a postwar intelligence service

At the end of the war, J. Edgar Hoover submitted his own plan for a central intelligence agency. Donovan's plan, which was much broader based and more inclusive of covert action, radio intercept, and propaganda, was eventually accepted by the United States government.

reporting directly to the President, staffed by OSS personnel who were already trained for such an undertaking. The OSS should not be disbanded, Donovan advised.

While Donovan's confidential report was still being digested by Roosevelt, the contents were deliberately leaked to arouse a bitter personal attack on Donovan and a storm of political acrimony around Roosevelt. The document was leaked by J. Edgar Hoover, Director of the FBI and a long-standing enemy of OSS, who saw an opportunity for damaging his opponent's chances of forming a rival peacetime service.

Donovan was denounced in thundering attacks from the press and the political arena, both of which accused him of proposing "an all powerful intelli-

After the war Donovan (shown here with W. Averell Harriman on the left and John McCloy in the middle) was very disappointed he was not named DCI. However, he continued to push for greater intelligence collection.

At left, General Donovan presents the Medal for Merit—the highest honor the United States could bestow to a non-American—to Sir William Stephenson, wartime head of British secret intelligence in the Western Hemisphere. Colonel Edward Buxton, assistant OSS director, looks on.

gence service to pry on the post-war world and to pry into the lives of citizens at home.''

The controversy escalated into violent diatribes which distorted Donovan's original memorandum. He was accused of "Gestapo" intentions.

Roosevelt quietly shelved further discussion of a peacetime intelligence service until a later date.

Six months later, at the beginning of April 1945, the President decided to revive Donovan's proposal. It was prepared for renewed consideration. But a week later Roosevelt was dead.

His successor, Harry Truman, wanted no part of Donovan's plan, and on October 1, 1945, OSS was disbanded.

Max Corvo, publisher of the *Middletown* (Connecticut) *Bulletin*, ran OSS operations against Italy during World War II. He is also director of the Symposium on the OSS. Max Corvo was awarded the Distinguished Service Medal, and probably more than any other OSS officer he participated in the full range of covert activities, including sabotage, propaganda, support of the underground, and management.

Q *How did you join OSS?*

A I came in via the army. I had written a secret plan for secret intelligence operations in Italy. OSS found out about it and recruited me. At first they thought I might be a provocation and had the counterespionage boys follow me for three days after I was sent to New York by Earl Brennan, head of my OSS unit.

Q *Because you were Italian?*

A Perhaps. Italy was at war and even the FBI followed Italians. Many Italians liked Mussolini before the war. But many more loved the U.S. and wanted to contribute.

Q *When did you run secret operations against Italy?*

A I joined OSS in 1942 and was later stationed in Algiers, where we set up administration offices, propaganda, and began planning to send men and materials into Italy and Sicily. Sardinia was also a target.

Q *Did we succeed in penetrating the Italian government during the war?*

A The government, the army, the Foreign Ministry, and other government departments.

Q *What about the Vatican. Did you penetrate it?*

A Yes.

Q *How did you operate?*

A First, I recruited hundreds of Sicilian-Americans for secret operations. Many were used behind the lines.

Q *In reading Earl Brennan's recommendation for your Distinguished Service Medal citation, Brennan states that you were the one responsible for establishing contacts with the underground, directing sabotage and covert operations, infiltrating teams into Italy, directing assault teams, collecting intelligence, and at the end of the war directing the capture of Fascist leaders. What do you regard as the most important?*

A It's hard to say. perhaps the prevention of large-scale destruction of northern Italy. All these efforts were essential to the United States winning the war.

Q *Was the Mafia instrumental in helping the U.S. landings?*

A They were almost nonexistent. Hundreds of Italian-Americans served, and many sacrificed their lives. None had Mafia connections. The Mafia stories are created by writers who do no research.

Q *Was the FBI suspicious of your activities during the war?*

A Yes. It was natural because we were at war with Italy. Sometimes they tailed my men.

Q *What about covert operations?*

A We dropped supplies, agents, and officers, supplied partisan groups, and helped shorten the war by months. We ran 24 clandestine radio stations that transmitted 125,000 cipher groups per month. We dropped more than 1 million pounds of materiel—weapons, food, et cetera. We trained the Italian underground. Men like Captain E.Q. Daddario captured Fascist leaders like Marshal Rudolfo Graziani and other ministers. We also constantly collected political and military intelligence.

INTELLIGENCE HIGHLIGHT

Rockefeller Center—HOME OF SPIES

Rockefeller Center, the New York City office and shopping complex, was a beehive of spies during World War II. Nelson Rockefeller, chairman of the State Department's Committee to Coordinate Inter-American Affairs, operated a vast intelligence gathering network for Latin America. Even before William Donovan became director of the OSS, Nelson Rockefeller with FBI backing received President Roosevelt's assurances that the OSS would stay out of Latin America. Rockefeller controlled intelligence units in Latin America from offices in the center. A few floors away, Sir William Stephenson ("Intrepid") operated suites of offices containing what was called the British Security Services—British intelligence in the United States. These offices comprised counterintelligence, propaganda, undercover operations, and coordination with OSS and the FBI for operations against Germany and Japan. One intelligence officer assigned to Stephenson from British Naval Intelligence was Ian Fleming, creator of superspy James Bond.

In his book *Casino Royale*, Fleming detailed how Bond killed a Japanese cipher clerk in the center. In reality, the Japanese government had a consular office on the 36th floor of Rockefeller Center. This office was one floor below the British Security Service's main office. The British knew that coded messages were being transmitted to Tokyo from this office. The office was broken into by two of Stephenson's agents and the code books were "borrowed" and microfilmed by Fleming. There the real story ended until Fleming let Bond do more in *Casino Royale*. However, an incident did take place in which a member of the Japanese delegation died.

Fleming in 1941 received from William Donovan a .38 caliber Colt Special with a note from Donovan—"FOR SPECIAL SERVICES." Fleming first claimed that he received the gift as a result of helping Donovan set up the OSS charter and organizational plan. However, Fleming later claimed to friends he had in fact killed the Japanese agent with a sandbag, and Donovan appreciated the deed and gave him the Colt. Research revealed that a Japanese citizen was accidentally killed by a "construction sandbag" crashing through his office window in 1941. Rockefeller Center did replace a large window on the 36th floor that year. An oldtimer who was there at the time remembered the "terrible accident—a large scaffold had crashed through the window and bashed this man to death." After the incident, the Japanese vacated those offices.

What with Rockefeller Center having once housed American, British, and Japanese spies, the center's connection to espionage is very strong. Many years after the war, and after Donovan's death, Donovan's law firm moved into the center. Today, a number of former OSS and CIA personnel still work in the center.

Establishing the C.I.A.

Establishing

THE CIA SEAL

Section 2 of the Central Intelligence Agency Act of 1949 provided for a seal of office for CIA. The design of the seal was approved and set forth on 17 February 1950 in President Truman's Executive Order 10111.

In Executive Order 10111, the CIA seal is described in heraldic terms as follows:

SHIELD: Argent, a compass rose of sixteen points.

CREST: On a wreath argent and gules an American bald eagle's head erased proper.

Below the shield on a gold color scroll the inscription "United States of America" in red letters, and encircling the shield and crest at the top the inscription "Central Intelligence Agency" in white letters.

All on a circular blue background with a narrow gold edge.

The interpretation of the CIA seal is as follows:

The American Eagle is the national bird and is a symbol of strength and alertness.

The radiating spokes of the compass rose depict the coverage of intelligence data from all areas of the world to a central point.

the C.I.A.

The Ames building serves as administrative and personnel offices for CIA. It is located in Rosslyn, Virginia.

The Central Intelligence Agency came into existence in 1947. For the first time in American history, a peacetime intelligence agency was given official recognition and formally acknowledged to be a necessary arm of government service in a politically volatile world.

Its formation followed the demise of OSS, a wartime espionage and intelligence service which had operated under the dynamic leadership of William J. Donovan. When it disbanded, its functions were absorbed by the State and War Departments. Almost a year prior to that Donovan had stated his beliefs in the need of a postwar centralized intelligence service. An organization, Donovan proposed, "which will produce intelligence both by overt and covert methods and will, at the same time, provide intelligence guidance, determine national intelligence objectives, and correlate the intelligence material collated by all government agencies."

He also suggested that this agency have authority to conduct "subversive operations abroad" but "no police or law enforcement functions either at home or abroad."

Donovan's plan drew heavy fire. The military services generally opposed a complete merger. The State Department thought it would supervise all peacetime operations affecting foreign relations. The FBI supported a system whereby military intelligence worldwide would be handled by the armed services and all civilian activities under its own jurisdiction.

<u>OSS terminated</u> by Executive Order 9621
Effective 1 October 1945

<u>Disposition of OSS functions,
personnel and assets</u>

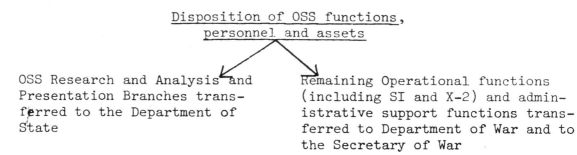

OSS Research and Analysis and
Presentation Branches trans-
ferred to the Department of
State

Remaining Operational functions
(including SI and X-2) and administrative support functions transferred to Department of War and to
the Secretary of War

[About 8,000 OSS personnel, both military and civilian, left the organization
following the end of the War. Of the elements transferred to the Department
of State, many ultimately left; those remaining became the intelligence organization of the Department of State (today known as the Bureau of Intelligence and Research). Of the OSS elements transferred to the War Department,
and renamed the Strategic Services Unit (SSU), again many of the military and
civilian personnel gradually were reassigned or left for private life. The
paramilitary units were disestablished. In the late fall of 1946, SSU began
to be transferred into the newly established Central Intelligence Group, and
from thence into the Central Intelligence Agency. This brought in many of
the old OSS'ers; others began to come to CIA from 1950 on.]

By Presidential Directive, dated January 22, 1946, President Truman established the

NATIONAL INTELLIGENCE AUTHORITY,

consisting of the Secretaries of State, War, and the Navy, and a personal representative of the President (Fleet Admiral William D. Leahy); assisted by
the

CENTRAL INTELLIGENCE GROUP.

The latter was headed by a Director of Central Intelligence, designated by
the President.

The formation of this initial peacetime intelligence organization was
preceded for over a year by much, often bitter, internecine debate between
the military intelligence services, the State Department, OSS, and the FBI.

In response to this policy debate, President Harry S Truman established the Central Intelligence Group in January 1946, directing it to coordinate existing departmental intelligence, supplementing but not supplanting their services. This was all to be done under the direction of the National Intelligence Authority composed of a Presidential representative and the Secretaries of State, War, and Navy. Rear Admiral Sidney W. Souers, USNR, who was the Deputy Chief of Naval Intelligence, was appointed the first Director of Central Intelligence. Air Force Lieutenant General Hoyt Vandenberg succeeded Souers as Director of the CIG in June 1946 and served until May 1947, when he turned the agency over to Rear Admiral Roscoe Hillenkoetter.

Under the provisions of the National Security Act of 1947 (which became effective on 18 September 1947) the National Security Council and the Central Intelligence Agency were established.

Larry Houston, who served for many years as CIA's general counsel, and his principal associate John Warner were the staff officers mainly responsible for drafting legislation for the new CIA. Walter Pforzheimer, CIG's legislative counsel, was the group's representative on Capitol Hill. These three men have for many years been major sources for the early history of CIA.

Most of the state's specific assignments given to the newly formed CIA, as well as the prohibitions on police and internal security functions, closely con-

Walter Pforzheimer (left) and Lawrence Houston are regarded as the leading experts on early CIA history.

formed to the concept of Donovan's original charter.

The 1947 Act charged the CIA with coordinating the nation's intelligence activities and correlating, evaluating, and disseminating intelligence which affects national security. In addition the Agency was to perform such other duties and functions relating to intelligence as the NSC might direct. The Act also made the DCI responsible for protecting intelligence sources and methods.

It was further stated that both the Director and the Deputy Director of Central Intelligence were to be appointed by the President, subject to confirmation by the Senate. An amendment of 4 April 1953 authorized such appointments to be made either from individuals in civilian life or from commissioned officers of the armed services, either in active or retired status, provided that "at no time shall the two positions . . . be occupied simultaneously by commissioned officers."

In 1949, the Central Intelligence Agency Act was passed supplementing the 1947 Act. Congress enacted additional provisions permitting the Agency to use confidential fiscal and administrative procedures and exempting CIA from many of the usual limitations on the expenditure of federal funds. It provided that CIA funds could be included in the budgets of other departments and then be transferred to the Agency without regard to the restrictions placed on the initial appropriation. This Act is the statutory authority for the secrecy of the agency's budget.

Riverside Stadium

2430 E Street

Yards and Docks

Quarters "Eye"

Curry Hall

Central Building

In addition to these buildings the CIA maintains offices in many U.S. cities and uses a number of military bases for training, language courses, tradecraft, and laboratories.

Tempo "Y"

2210 E Street

J. Edgar Hoover, Harry Truman, and Attorney General J. Howard McGrath discuss intelligence matters in the United States. Hoover continued to lobby for one intelligence service under his direction.

In order to further protect intelligence sources and methods from disclosure, the 1949 Act further exempted the CIA from having to disclose its "organization, functions, names, officials, titles, salaries or numbers of personnel employees."

The authority of the CIA was clearly established. Only J. Edgar Hoover, head of the FBI, raised the persistent voice of dissension and insisted that material from his agency's files would be made available *only* on written request.

CIA was a peacetime agency but war-related factors were always to the fore. In addition to the collection and analysis of clandestine intelligence, the agency now began to play a forceful role in covert psychological and political areas.

Between 1945 and 1948 the Soviet Union seized military and political control in most of Eastern Europe and threatened to do the same in Greece, Turkey, Iran, Yugoslavia, and Berlin.

Italy was seen as a key, strategic point to a secure position in the Mediterranean, and a private document issued by the National Security Council proposed that "the United States should as a matter of priority immediately undertake further measures designed to prevent the Communists from winning participation in the Government." President Truman endorsed the practice of providing covert assistance for those who opposed Communist aims. The CIA provided financial and technical assistance to the Christian Democrats and other anti- or non-

The lobby of the new CIA addition.

Communist parties for the April 1949 elections, which ended in triumph for these parties.

Following this successful covert action in Italy, George Kennan, Director of the State Department's Policy Planning Staff, advocated the formal creation of a permanent covert political action department that would include paramilitary operations as well as political and economic warfare. It was named the Office of Policy Coordination (OPC) and was headed by Frank Wisner, the former OSS chief in Rumania.

Although covert actions were not specifically included in the original principles of law, they were considered to be covered by a catchall phrase that referred to "such other functions and duties related to intelligence affecting the national security as the

A meeting of the National Security Council.

National Security Council may from time to time direct.''

In addition to providing funds and information for non-Communist parties, publications, groups, and other important individual voices throughout Eastern Europe, the CIA also made extensive use of radio, providing accurate news and political analysis through Radio Free Europe and, in the Soviet Union itself, Radio Liberty.

While the European effort was mainly political and information-oriented, the Asian area of concern in the early 1950s became the target of paramilitary operations. Many thousands of troops had been left behind in remote areas of southwestern China after the Nationalist Chinese retreated to Taiwan in 1949. The

CIA set out to impede the Chinese fighting in Korea and supported paramilitary efforts with increasing numbers of aircraft and boats and a heavy network of agents.

Korea engendered a quasi-wartime situation that intensified the need for better intelligence and focused attention on the CIA, centering it in a position of prominence.

The CIA gained added distinction with the arrival of General Walter Bedell Smith as Director. He replaced Hillenkoetter in October 1950.

Smith already had a prestigious reputation. He had served as Chief of Staff to General Eisenhower throughout the European war, and had later been appointed ambassador to the USSR, an experience

The Shah of Iran was installed with the aid of CIA. This successful operation established the CIA as a superb arm of the President's foreign policy.

that was to serve him well in his dealings with intelligence experts in the Soviet Union.

For the first time since Donovan, central intelligence was seen to be in the hands of a consummate professional and a commanding presence; a man who had the support of Truman and a capability for persuasive communication with military and political leaders. General Walter Bedell Smith imposed a pattern on the CIA that remained virtually unchanged for 20 years.

William H. Jackson became Deputy Director of Central Intelligence and Allen Dulles, then in private law practice after his years in OSS, was brought back into the intelligence profession.

From the military Smith recruited men like General Clarence Huebner, who commanded the First Infantry Division for much of the combat phase of World War II in Europe, and General Harold Bull who had served with Smith in SHAEF G3 (Operations) and was a brilliant analyst.

Now growing in stature, the CIA gained a further tribute to its reputation when it came to the aid of the Shah of Iran, who had been driven from his country by his left-leaning premier, Mohammed Mossadegh. The CIA mounted a counterattack against Mossadegh, who was supported by the local Communist party and the Soviet Union. It hired demonstrators to intimidate Mossadegh supporters and instructed the Shah's

Under General Walter Bedell Smith's direction, the CIA became organized and a functioning arm of the United States government.

Here, General Smith, the new CIA director Allen Dulles, and General Omar Bradley after leaving the White House.

loyal military forces in methods of taking over the local radio station, paving a way for their ruler's triumphant return.

Of all CIA activities, General Smith assessed the dissemination of national estimates to be the most difficult and the most important. Smith created the Office of National Estimates and removed this field of operations entirely from day to day developments to concentrate specifically on the production of intelligence projections. William Langer, the Harvard historian, was appointed head of ONE, and Yale historian Sherman Kent was made his deputy. Both had served in the OSS Research and Analysis Branch.

Smith had clear requirements of his staff. He wanted a daily intelligence report to be made available to the President which clearly summarized the most important developments in the world affecting U.S. interests. The intensive report was to be completely analyzed and evaluated by top experts round the clock, 24 hours a day, 7 days a week.

Representatives of all offices participated in preparation of the reports. They included OCI, the Office of Current Intelligence, which had built up a cadre of analysts greatly familiar with all sources of data; ORR, the Office of Research and Reports, which provided in-depth studies on geographic characteristics of all foreign territories; OSI, the Office of Scientific Intelligence, a more specialized group of analysts possessing considerable knowledge in the fields of atomic energy and missile technology.

Central Intelligence Agency
1953

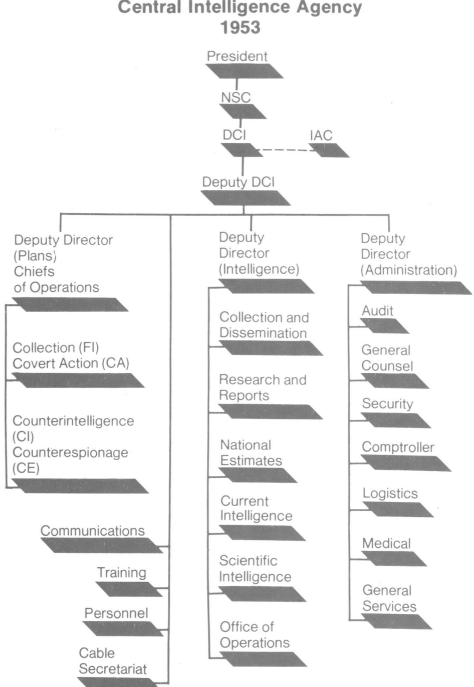

President

NSC

DCI   IAC

Deputy DCI

Deputy Director (Plans) Chiefs of Operations

Collection (FI) Covert Action (CA)

Counterintelligence (CI) Counterespionage (CE)

Communications

Training

Personnel

Cable Secretariat

Deputy Director (Intelligence)

Collection and Dissemination

Research and Reports

National Estimates

Current Intelligence

Scientific Intelligence

Office of Operations

Deputy Director (Administration)

Audit

General Counsel

Security

Comptroller

Logistics

Medical

General Services

Allen Dulles, a CIA case officer, and Ray Cline on their round-the-world trip visiting CIA stations in 1956.

Information is gathered and disseminated to experts in different offices, resulting in a complete sharing of all information among the agencies so that everyone works from the same set of facts. The overall responsibility for the daily report to the President was assigned to the Office of National Estimates. It became known as the "Daily."

By 1953 the personnel strength of CIA had multiplied from a few hundred to around 10,000 in number. In three years General Walter Bedell Smith had transformed the CIA and brought about the necessary changes to enable it to become an effective service.

By the time Smith became Secretary of State and Allen Dulles became Director of Central Intelligence in February 1953, the CIA had begun to take the form Donovan visualized so long before.

Organization of the C.I.A.

Organization

of the C.I.A.

Director of Central Intelligence Command Responsibilities

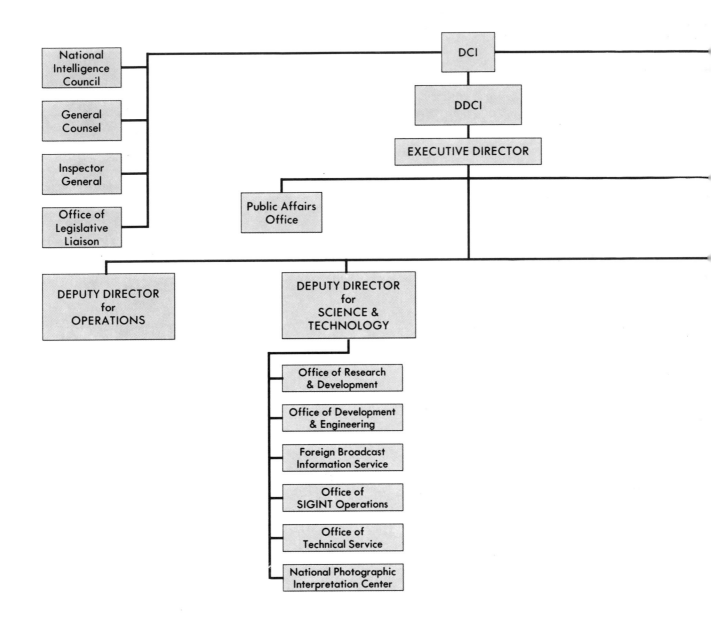

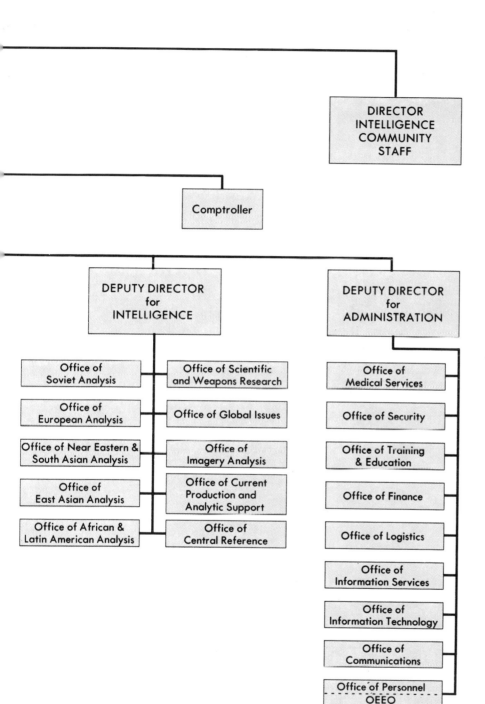

DIRECTOR
INTELLIGENCE
COMMUNITY
STAFF

Comptroller

DEPUTY DIRECTOR for INTELLIGENCE

Office of Soviet Analysis

Office of European Analysis

Office of Near Eastern & South Asian Analysis

Office of East Asian Analysis

Office of African & Latin American Analysis

Office of Scientific and Weapons Research

Office of Global Issues

Office of Imagery Analysis

Office of Current Production and Analytic Support

Office of Central Reference

DEPUTY DIRECTOR for ADMINISTRATION

Office of Medical Services

Office of Security

Office of Training & Education

Office of Finance

Office of Logistics

Office of Information Services

Office of Information Technology

Office of Communications

Office of Personnel
OEEO

The CIA has had many organizational structures since it was established in 1947. The organization has changed usually to meet new and different requirements in a constantly changing world. The Central Intelligence Agency Act of 1949 exempts the CIA from publishing or disclosing its setup in the interests of protecting the nature of the agency's functions. From time to time since 1975, however, the CIA and Congress have officially made public the basic organization of the CIA. What follows is an office-by-office breakdown of the current known structure.

The Headquarters Building

Located about eight miles from downtown Washington, D.C., the headquarters building and grounds presently occupied by the Central Intelligence Agency were envisioned by former Director Allen W. Dulles. His concept, projecting the atmosphere of a college campus, was designed in the mid-1950's by the New York firm of Harrison and Abramovitz—designers of the United Nations building.

Construction began in October 1957 and was completed in November 1963. President Dwight D. Eisenhower laid the building's cornerstone on November 3, 1959.

The Central Intelligence Agency Headquarters, actually commissioned by President Harry S Truman, consists of 1,000,000 square feet. When combined, the building and the grounds surrounding it total 219 acres. Concrete and Georgia marble make up the main lobby and corridor. Along the south corridor are messages of gratitude and approbation to the Central Intelligence Agency from Presidents Truman, Eisenhower, Kennedy, Johnson, Nixon, Ford and Carter.

A Biblical verse, which characterizes the intelligence mission in a free society, is etched into the south wall of the central lobby. It reads:

And ye shall know the truth and the truth shall make you free.

John VIII-XXXII

Opposite, on the north wall of the central lobby, is a bas-relief bust of Allen Welsh Dulles who was Director of the Central Intelligence Agency for nine years. The building was erected during his period in office.

Engraved in the same wall are memorial stars, each honoring a Central Intelligence Agency employee whose life was lost in the service of our country. For security reasons the names of many of these dedicated Americans can never be revealed.

The **Director of Central Intelligence** (DCI) is the primary national foreign intelligence advisor to the President and the National Security Council (NSC). His responsibilities are detailed throughout this book.

The **Deputy Director of Central Intelligence** (DDCI) is appointed by the President, with the advice and consent of the Senate, to act for and exercise the powers of the DCI during his absence or disability. The DCI and DDCI usually divide the numerous duties of the DCI between them as the DCI decides. Among his duties, the DDCI represents the CIA on the National Foreign Intelligence Board (NFIB).

The **Executive Director** (EXDIR) is appointed by the DCI to act for the DCI and the DDCI in the overall daily management of the CIA. He coordinates the activities of the several components and oversees the development and execution of the CIA's annual program.

The **Director Intelligence Community Staff** (D/ICS) is appointed by the DCI to head an interagency staff that assists the DCI in carrying out his function as the senior intelligence officer responsible for a coordinated, national intelligence effort by the intelligence community. Personnel from all the concerned agencies are assigned to the staff. A 1982 organizational chart listed the following offices as part of the ICS: Assessment and Evaluation, Community Coordination, HUMINT Collection, Imagery Collection and Exploitation, SIGINT Collection, Planning, and Program and Budget Coordination.

The **Comptroller** is responsible for the planning, programming, and budgeting of the CIA. The function also includes the development and maintenance of financial control systems.

The **Public Affairs Office** serves as the point of contact for the public in general and the news media in particular. The office provides some unclassified CIA studies and arranges media, academic, and business contacts with appropriate CIA personnel on a variety of subjects.

The **National Intelligence Council** produces the National Intelligence Estimate (NIE), which the DCI submits to the President, NSC, and other designated elements of the executive branch. While the NIE is considered to be the DCI's views on a given subject, it actually is the result of an interagency effort.

The **General Counsel** is the principal legal officer of the CIA. He provides legal advice to the DCI and legal counsel and guidance to employees at all levels within the CIA on issues concerning the legality and propriety of the CIA's activities, so that such activities are consistent with the Constitution and laws of the United States and applicable executive orders and CIA rules and regulations. The General Counsel also reviews proposed legislation and directives affecting CIA activities. The office also monitors CIA adherence to the Freedom of Information and Privacy Acts and provides legal advice to the CIA's Publications Review Board, which reviews the writings of former and current CIA, employees for possible breaches of security. The General Counsel is always alert for violations of the U.S. Criminal Code, which are reported to the Department of Justice, and for impropriety or illegality, which is reported to the Intelligence Oversight Board.

The **Inspector General** (IG) is the investigative arm of the DCI and assists him and the heads of offices and directorates in improving the performance of CIA offices and personnel. The IG endeavors to assure that CIA activities are consistent with all the laws and regulations that govern them. The IG conducts inspections of all CIA components to examine how well each carries out its function, whether organizational changes are in order, and the quality and performance of the personnel involved. He also makes special investigations and studies as directed by the DCI.

The **Office of Legislative Liaison** is responsible for the CIA's liaison with Congress, particularly the Senate and House Select Committees on Intelligence. The office tries to meet congressional needs by answering queries, arranging appearances of appropriate CIA officers at public or executive hearings, arranging visits by members of Congress and/or their staffs to CIA installations, and in general staying in close touch with the members and committees of Congress to forestall or minimize the possibility of unnecessary clashes between the CIA and Congress.

The **Deputy Director for Science and Technology** (DDS&T) is appointed by the DCI. The directorate researches and develops technical collection systems. To stay abreast of scientific and technical developments, the directorate has constant interchange with the scientific and industrial communities.

The **Office of Research and Development** (R&D) conducts basic and applied scientific and technical research and development in a wide variety of fields, including chemistry, computer science, aeronautics, photogrammetry, and communications, among many others. This office works closely with the **Office of Development and Engineering** (D&E), which is responsible for designing and operating technical collection systems.

The **Foreign Broadcast Information Service** (FBIS), a service of common concern, operates a worldwide newtork of broadcast monitoring units responsible for reviewing the foreign media. The information to be translated and disseminated to consumers is selected based on a set of intelligence requirements from the consumers. The bulk of the FBIS product is unclassified and is published in a "Daily Report" for a particular geographic area, and it is available to the public for a fee from the National Technical Information Service (NTIS) of the U.S. Department of Commerce.

The **Office of SIGINT Operations** collects information on all communications intelligence, electronics intelligence, and foreign instrumentation (telemetry) signals intelligence, however transmitted. This office plays a supporting role to the National Security Agency.

The **Office of Technical Service** (OTS) is responsible for technical research, development, and engineering of items particularly related to clandestine activities. Not all of the James Bond type of gadgetry is possible in the real world, but some of it must be considered to be at least in the realm of possibility.

The **National Photographic Interpretation Center** (NPIC) is another service of common concern under the overall direction of the DCI. It is staffed by personnel from the CIA and the military services and is responsible for analyzing photography derived from overhead reconnaissance for the benefit of the entire intelligence community.

The **Deputy Director for Intelligence** (DDI) is responsible for the analysis and production of "finished national intelligence" encompassing foreign political intelligence, international economic intelligence, foreign scientific and weapons and related military intelligence, and numerous other subjects of interest to the President and policymakers. "Finished national intelligence" is the integration, evaluation, and assessment of events abroad that draws its source material, of whatever classification, from all the intelligence collection systems and programs of the government. Because the DDI and the directorate—in theory, at least—have no responsibility or loyalty to any particular department, such as State or Defense or Treasury, and are not responsible for making policy decisions or advocating one policy over another, the DDI can produce truly objective analysis and reporting for use by the President and his advisors in formulating foreign and national security policy. The DDI is responsible for the production of CIA's input to the National Intelligence Estimate produced by the National Intelligence Council. The DDI represents the DCI in maters of substantive intelligence in the NSC policy-making structure, in the executive branch at the cabinet level, with the Congress, with the academic and business worlds, and with the public.

The directorate is organized along both geographic and functional lines. The five geographic offices are the **Office of Soviet Analysis,** the **Office of European Analysis,** the **Office of Near East and South Asian Analysis,** the **Office of East Asian Analysis,** and the **Office of African and Latin American Analysis.** The offices conduct political, economic, military, sociological, biographic, and other analysis of all countries in their respective geographic areas.

The **Office of Scientific and Weapons Research** (OSWR) analyzes the technical aspects of foreign weapons and space systems. This includes their design, production, maintenance, performance characteristics, deployment capabilities, and technical endurance. In addition, OSWR analyzes and prepares studies on nuclear weapons, nuclear energy, nuclear proliferation, technology transfer (particularly from the U.S. and its allies to the Soviet Union), tactical and general-purpose weapons, strategic forces, offensive and defensive strategic weapons systems, antisubmarine weapons, scientific policy, and physical and life sciences.

The **Office of Global Issues** analyzes international economic, geographic, and technological issues, including international trade, development, and commodity markets. It also analyzes and reports on such special topics as international terrorism, narcotics production and movement, weapons transfer, and political instability around the world.

The **Office of Imagery Analysis** produces intelligence assessments based on analysis and interpretation of photography and similar technical sources. The subjects covered are numerous, including industrial and agricultural production, movement of military forces, and weapons development, testing, production, and deployment.

The **Office of Current Production and Analytic Support** publishes all DDI intelligence reports. It also researches and compiles data leading to the preparation of CIA special subject maps, charts, and graphics for use in CIA reports and briefings. The CIA's 24-hour Operations Center is also the responsibility of this office. Analytic support is manifested in providing analysts with help in mathematical statistics, operations research, econometrics, and political methodology.

The **Office of Central Reference** produces biographic intelligence on foreign personalities and organizations, maintains a vast collection of foreign and domestic publications and documents in support of intelligence research, receives and disseminates a variety of intelligence reports and studies, operates special libraries containing maps, documents, photographic materials, unclassified books, newspapers, and periodicals, maintains extensive computer programs for storage, retrieval, and dissemination of information, and has computer links to data banks throughout the country and the world.

The **Deputy Director for Administration** (DDA) provides the multitude of normal housekeeping details that go with any large organization, such as finance, medical services, communications, training, and security for the CIA's personnel and facilities. The DDA also provides the same services to those elements of the intelligence community outside CIA but under the jurisdiction of the DCI.

The **Office of Medical Services** (OMS) is responsible for the CIA's medical program, which includes medical examination of new employees, periodic medical examination of all employees, preventive medicine, emergency health care, psychiatric diagnosis and advice, and medical support in operations and intelligence production. The office also maintains an overseas medical program in support of CIA personnel and activities abroad.

The **Office of Security** (OS) is responsible for programs to protect CIA personnel, facilities, and activities at home and abroad. The office investigates employment applicants, conducts periodic polygraph examinations, issues a variety of clearances, engages in a variety of activities to ensure physical security, and is also concerned with computer security among other security matters.

The **Office of Training and Education** (OTE) provides training courses to all CIA employees. This includes training in intelligence collection and production, foreign languages, writing, speaking, and research, and arranging for external training in other government and nongovernment institutions. The office also gives refresher courses on specific subjects to employees who need them and produces classified and unclassified monographs on a variety of intelligence subjects.

The **Office of Finance** (OF) is responsible for monetary matters, including budgeting, accounting, auditing, payroll, and support to overseas activities (including the procurement of foreign currency). It is the watchdog for CIA's funds.

The **Office of Logistics** (OL) provides land, buildings, and facilities for CIA's people and activities, procures supplies from pens and pencils to aircraft, transports people and equipment wherever they must go, prints and binds CIA reports and studies, an in general oversees the contracting for the entire range of facilities and services needed to support CIA activities.

The **Office of Information Services** (OIS) develops and maintains systems for storage and retrieval of information in all its forms in support of all the various parts of the CIA. This involves both manual and computer-based systems at home and abroad. This office works closely with the **Office of Information Technology** (OIT), which develops and operates sophisticated information-processing facilities.

The **Office of Communications** (OC) provides electronic communications facilities for CIA activities worldwide. This includes, but is not limited to, cable facilities, agent radios, and microwave and satellite equipment.

The **Office of Personnel** (OP) maintains a nationwide recruiting system, including evaluation, promotion, and assignment policies, development of staffing and management procedures, and operation of an employee benefits and services program. Closely connected to this office is the **Office of Equal Employment Opportunity** (OEEO), which ensures according to the law that no discrimination occurs against employees or applicants.

The **Deputy Director for Operations** (DDO) is responsible for the clandestine collection of foreign intelligence (usually by human agents), for conducting counterintelligence abroad, and for engaging in "special activities" or clandestine activities conducted abroad to influence opinion and events in support of U.S. foreign policy objectives. These latter activities, sometimes called "covert action", ideally are executed so that the role of the U.S. government is not apparent or publicly acknowledged. It is this directorate that comes to mind whenever the public sees the initials CIA in print or on television. As the organizational chart shows, there is no official breakdown for this component, which is also called the Clandestine Service.

Based on previously released information, it can be assumed that this directorate is organized along both geographic and functional lines. The geographic units may be organized along the regional breakdown used by the DDI. The geographic units, called "area divisions", are responsible for establishing and supporting their units in the field, called "stations", the bulk of which are located abroad. Those few units in the United States deal with Americans who have information on foreign areas that they wish to share with the CIA and support those foreign persons temporarily on American soil who want to assist the CIA.

The units organized along functional lines are called "staffs" and again, if the past is any guide, are probably organized as specialists to assist in clandestine collection, counterintelligence, and special activities. The latter may also include special units for political and psychological operations, economic activities, and, of course, paramilitary activities. These probably vary with demand. While the actual organizational chart of the DDO will vary from time to time, the basic geographic area and functional staff arrangement has remained constant.

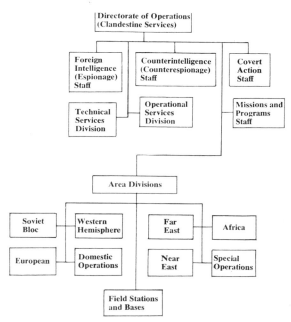

CARTOGRAPHY, AND CRATEOLOGY

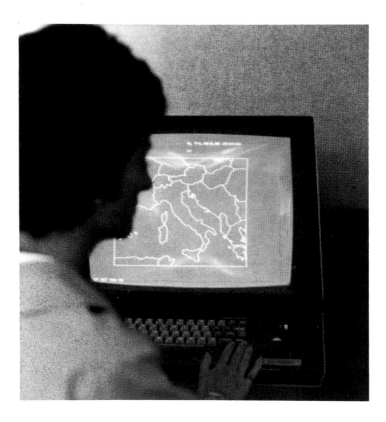

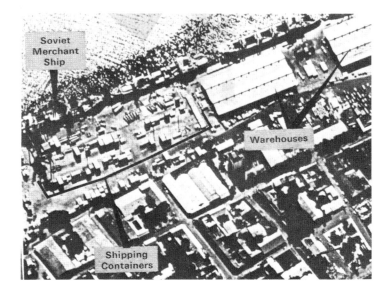

Cartography

The CIA's cartography department is probably the best in the world. With information gathered from agents and satellites the CIA has been able to create a variety of accurate and well-documented maps—many available to the public. Foreign powers as well as social scientists have benefited for years by using CIA maps of agriculture, minerals, oil, coastlines, fishing areas, and so forth. Locations of military and training bases are also occasionally released to the public. Maps created for secret use are of items such as street maps of Communist countries, terrorist training bases, troop movements, ship movements, and military maneuvers. Vigilance of military moves, especially during a crisis between superpowers, helps leaders make decisions that can avoid war or continued confrontation.

Crateology

When the Soviets attempted to ship war supplies to Cuba in the 1960s, the CIA decided that it needed more information on what was in the crates. Since that time, and more recently with new arms shipments to Nicaragua, Afghanistan, and Angola, the CIA developed a new department, one to study crates. Although satellites can photograph crates on ships and sometimes detect (through cracks) the objects in the crates, new information was needed. What type of wood, how the crate is constructed, and its dimensions are all studied to know whether the crate is carrying an offensive missile able to hit the United States, a new MiG fighter, or electronic gear. Crateology is now divided into the following categories: ammunition, aircraft, missiles, tanks, nuclear materials, and trucks.

CAVEOLOGY, CHRONOLOGY,

Besides the specialized areas of science, technology, history, economics, and other scholarly disciplines, the CIA maintains a unique variety of capabilities necessary to intelligence decision-making and to field agents. Here are a few examples.

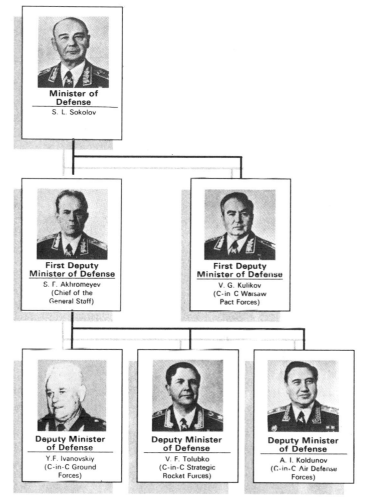

Caveology

The CIA has long maintained a specialized department that constructs models, dioramas, and the like of terra firma. It collects intelligence from satellites, agents on the ground, and spy planes. It then illustrates the intelligence and the model-makers go to work. Streets in Moscow, dams in Latin America, and beaches and buildings are all subjects for the model-makers. At one time the agency had scale models of more than 600 caves in Cuba. These caves at one time were used as the offices and storage sites for Fidel Castro. These models enable possible agent teams to locate hiding places or possible storage depots. Besides the caves, secret underground sites or changes in, say, a street in Moscow are all topics. The Soviets issue false maps to confuse spies but they confuse their own citizens as well. The CIA is rarely confused as it constantly updates its models.

Chronology

Both the DIA and the CIA jointly collect information on the leaders of the Soviet Union. Because it is difficult to obtain information on Soviet leaders, a number of methods must be developed. The best is to have agents who have access to the Soviet leadership. Because it is often difficult for Americans to operate in the Soviet Union, the next best way is to identify anyone who may have contact with Soviet leaders. Their history, their work habits, the way they think, their personal habits and psychological makeup are all targets of interest. Over the years the Soviets have accused the CIA of bugging the cars of the Politburo and the offices of the Soviet government, and recruiting Soviet citizens, especially dissidents, to spy. What is known is that the biographical information gathered has played an important role in decision-making at summits and other confrontations between the U.S. and USSR.

Definition and Mission of the C.I.A.

Definition and Mission of the C.I.A.

Intelligence activities, particularly the collection and analysis of information, have been engaged in by man from time immemorial. Peoples and then nations have risen and fallen depending on how well they acquired and used the information they needed to survive. The Old Testament tells of the Lord instructing Moses to "Send thee men, that they may search the land of Canaan" and that Moses sent 12 men "to spy out the land," and later Joshua sent 2 men "to spy secretly" on Jericho. But while this and other references usually emphasize the exotic use of spies or other secret sources, intelligence has always meant far more than that, and this is especially so in today's world. The overwhelming amount of information collected derives from (1) open sources such as books, periodicals, newspapers, radio and television broadcasts, government documents, governmental statements, academic and commercial studies, et cetera, and (2) data collected by technical means such as photographic and signals intelligence. To this vast base of knowledge is then added the small but often vital amount of information obtained clandestinely by human agents or spies, an activity called espionage.

In addition to the collection and analysis of information, intelligence activities also include counterintelligence and covert action. All these activities were engaged in by the American colonies even before they declared their independence in 1776. In 1775, the Second Continental Congress established

The Nathan Hale statue outside headquarters in Langley.

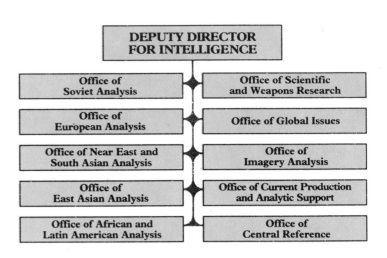

DEPUTY DIRECTOR FOR INTELLIGENCE	
Office of Soviet Analysis	Office of Scientific and Weapons Research
Office of European Analysis	Office of Global Issues
Office of Near East and South Asian Analysis	Office of Imagery Analysis
Office of East Asian Analysis	Office of Current Production and Analytic Support
Office of African and Latin American Analysis	Office of Central Reference

the first official American intelligence organizations with the creation of the Secret Committee and then the Committee of Secret Correspondence. George Washington himself engaged in intelligence activity, often directing intelligence requirements, managing intelligence and counterintelligence agents, and directing psychological warfare campaigns and deception operations, and he made his own estimates of the situation. It was not until World War II, however, that the United States began to establish a national coordinated intelligence service.

The CIA, which was established in 1947, was given the mission of "coordinating the intelligence activities of the several Government departments and agencies in the interest of national security." To accomplish its mission the CIA, under the direction of the National Security Council, was given the following functions:

(1) To advise the NSC on the intelligence activities of the government departments and agencies relating to national security;

(2) To make recommendations to the NSC for coordinating such governmental intelligence activities;

(3) To correlate, evaluate, and disseminate intelligence relating to national security with the specific provision that the government departments and agencies would continue to collect, evaluate, correlate, and disseminate departmental intelligence. It was clearly stated in the National Security Act of 1947

that the CIA was to "have no police, subpoena, law-enforcement powers, or internal-security functions." The act also provided that the DCI "shall be responsible for protecting intelligence sources and methods from unauthorized disclosure";

(4) To perform for the existing intelligence agencies such "services of common concern" that the NSC determines can be better done centrally;

(5) "To perform such other functions and duties relating to intelligence affecting the national security as the National Security Council may from time to time direct."

While functions **4** and **5** seem unclear and vague, it was not the fashion in 1947 for governments to state officially that they engaged in activities such as espionage. The record is clear, however, that those concerned with the passage of the National Security Act, including the members of Congress involved, clearly understood that the CIA would engage in espionage and counterintelligence as "services of common concern." The declassified transcript of the congressional hearings held behind closed doors at the time does not leave any room for doubt on that point. The meaning of function 5, however, was not as clear, nor was its meaning ever questioned, although similar language is found in the original 1944 Donovan plan and military proposals for the creation of a postwar centralized intelligence organization.

On June 20, 1949, Congress supplemented the 1947 act by passing the Central Intelligence Agency Act, which provided the CIA with several fiscal and administrative authorities. Among these are keeping secret the agency's budget and the numbers and names of its personnel, permitting CIA funds to be included in the budgets of other departments and then transferred to the CIA without the restrictions placed on the initial appropriation, and accounting for expenditures of funds solely on the certification of the DCI.

Under the 1947 and 1949 acts, the DCI serves as the principal advisor to the President and the NSC on all matters of foreign intelligence relating to the national security. The CIA's responsibilities are carried out subject to various directives and controls by the President and the NSC.

The CIA continues to function today as intelligence coordinator, producer of national foreign intelligence, provider of "services of common concern," and performer as an action arm in support of U.S. foreign policy.

THE CIA CASE OFFICER

A Central Intelligence Agency case officer usually reports to the chief of station and has a number of agents, almost always foreign-born, reporting to and working for him.

George didn't even roll over at six o'clock and he hadn't felt Joan slide out of the bed at seven to start the family routine with the children, because he'd just hit the sack at four-thirty. Long night . . . and morning, George had thought before sleep grabbed him.

George is a fairly typical CIA case officer or "operator" stationed anywhere between Rabat and Rangoon. He works the jobs of two men and never feels he completes the work of one. He rises (when he can) at about 8:00 A.M. to help Joan get the kids ready and off to school, then he sits a bit to unscramble last night and make his ever tentative plans for the day.

With or without George, Joan has gotten the kids off (having also pulled off George's other sock and shoe) and had coffee before jabbing him at 8:30. A former CIA analyst, Joan knows her husband's drill, knows that before "cover" work that morning he has to meet a cutout to pick up an agent's letter in secret writing.

But before meeting the cutout, George walks a countersurveillance course to assure himself that he drew no host-country surveillant's attention, which would compromise his live mail drop. This kind of premeeting shuffle takes time, so twenty minutes and one half cup of coffee later George is on the road.

George has no appetite but knows he has to eat, so he downs a pack of crackers. At 1:30 he has a meeting to brief and deliver a package to a Communist-country courier for dropping behind the iron curtain. Negotiating the enemy border with the small oddly configured cache and then "dead dropping" it could present problems if the courier is not properly briefed. If things don't go precisely, one or two lives might be lost. So, ever dedicated to precision, George goes over the concealment and caching drill twice. Boris needs this; he is good and reliable, but this particular Boris needs oral instructions. Paper instructions would never do.

And so with luck, George returns to the station by 3:30 P.M. And then the writing begins. There is the agent message to put into intelligence format and, of course, the quite different operational report to do for the field records file. What if George died tomorrow? How would his successor know where he had left off in this case? How could the agent be met again? Where? And are the pay accounts right? This is important: the agent's wife is dying of cancer and the Communist state mechanism for administering socialized care seems to be letting her die a socialized death on a socialized schedule. Care and compassion, George thought, are the basic elements of good agent handling. And George is good. Joan knows this, hating him for it when time and again he fouls up her social plans, but respecting and loving him for it, too.

And at 6:00 P.M. he has to stop again, because this is when, for tonight's small diplomatic gathering hosted by the Pakistani ambassador, he needs to devise the means to get Vladimir off to the side for more than 10 minutes this time. Vlad, a known Czech intelligence officer, seems to be fishing for something. Was it asylum in the West as the price for what he could tell CIA about his country's operations against the U.S.? Or, obviously much worse and very time consuming, would Vladimir be up to the common game of trying to lead him down the garden path to making a mistake that, in turn, might lead to his being thrown out of the host country? Through no fault of his own, George had already been thrown out of one country. None of this particularly helped Joan's state of health or the kids' educations, so he'd have to be on his guard. Was all this worth it? Lord, he'd been offered more by Sunoco to do much less!

THE CHIEF OF STATION

The chief of station is a career intelligence officer usually operating under cover in an American embassy. Chief of station is a Central Intelligence Agency title.

Wherever there is a CIA station, no matter how large or small, there is need for someone to run it. Who is he? What does he look like? What does he appear to do for a living to those uninformed about his true identity? What's his title and where does he stand in our embassy, military command locations, or any of the large number of U.S. government offices abroad? What does his day—and night—consist of?

First of all, he is the CIA Director's personal representative in any dealings he must have within or without the station structure. If, outside the secret councils of his station, he is to manage his representational and "cover" duties properly, he will need to deal with and frequently assist those diverse members of the U.S. government family that exist in any foreign country, for he is almost always a key member of the U.S. "country team" in that foreign location.

And, within the station, he must personally watch over the care, feeding, and close-in operational direction and follow-on execution and reporting of his case officers who work the street as well as the inside analysts and operational support people who constitute the administrative backbone of his command.

This is no one-or-two-hour-a-day chore. It is a constant watch, an almost unending vigil if one is to do it right. When his bedside signaling device alerts him at 3:00 A.M. that he has an "IMMEDIATE" (cable) waiting for him in his hidden communications center, he truly must rise and shine (however blearily), personally appearing as soon as possible at his command site to submit to the reporting requirements of his ever urgently disposed masters in Washington.

And if during normal (or even abnormal) working hours his ambassador summons him to give counsel or he receives an urgent personal visit from the leader of a friendly foreign intelligence or security service—if these kinds of things intervene, he must put aside in-station matters for short periods and do his "representational" thing, returning later—sometimes much later—to minister to the guidance needs of his command.

The prime functions of command in pursuit of intelligence goals are to inspire and lead a station complement into dangerous and frequently uncharted byways, where the very act of staying

unerringly on course verges on the debilitating. What this amounts to is guiding his station members in quest of a target country's most closely held and assiduously protected state secrets, stuff that one can't overhear or elicit at striped pants gatherings, material which cannot be researched in libraries or tracked down in the traditional manner of the Fourth Estate, stuff which can only be gotten through recruited, controlled, and ideologically committed secret sources or other technical or mechanical methods of information acquisition.

The nub of what these CIA station chiefs are after consists of facts giving notice that a certain foreign country's intentions or plans are such that might either hurt or otherwise adversely affect U.S. interests in critical areas or, at worst, actually threaten our national survival.

Such stuff is obviously hard to find, not to mention acquire, because it is normally restricted to the fewest number of eyes or ears and, therefore, if ever committed to paper or recording tape, is consigned to the deepest and most highly protected vaults in the enemy kingdom.

But in a game as exacting as collecting another country's most highly guarded secrets, the regimen is ever a chancy one. It demands constant and sometimes superhuman vigilance. For were a

chief of station ever to decentralize or otherwise relinquish responsibility for operational decision, were he to abdicate the exercise of fierce focus over the activities of his officers, he would not deserve the honor of the title, chief of station.

The best of the CIA's chiefs of station, who direct our nation's most critical operational commands, have had years of street experience of their own. In their green and middle years, they've worked the roads from Bombay to Berlin. They've worked in top hats and turbans, debriefed agents in taxis and tongas, and are as familiar with the back streets of Tripoli as they are with the dens of the Mafia in Rome's Trastevere. They speak, read, and write two or three foreign languages. They've run agents from the level of kiosk informer and taxi driver to an enemy country's foreign ministry official; they've placed microphones to listen to Communist agents discussing intentions against us, and they've sent agents deep into "denied areas" and maintained secret and safe contact with them for months, until able to pull them out to secret sites in the West to personally review their work and the agent mandate.

So, this is America's practicing chief of station —just in case you haven't ever been able to see one. Do you recognize him now?

INTERVIEW WITH CIA

Does the Central Intelligence Agency spy on Americans? Does it keep a file on me?

No. The Central Intelligence Agency is expressly prohibited by Presidential Executive Order from routinely engaging in the domestic use of such techniques as electronic, mail, or physical surveillance; monitoring devices; or unconsented physical search. Such intrusion into the lives of Americans by any Government agency could take place only under the most extraordinary conditions of concern for the national welfare and, even then, only when approved by the Attorney General. Similarly, the Agency does not maintain portfolios on private citizens. Names of American citizens may appear in various records as a consequence of routine business they conduct with the Agency, but they are in no way segregated for surveillance or special attention. Any citizen has the right to confirm this fact under the authority of the Privacy Act.

Who decides when the Central Intelligence Agency should engage in covert actions, and why?

Only the President can direct the Agency to undertake a covert action. Such actions are recommended by the National Security Council. Once tasked, the Director of Central Intelligence must notify the intelligence oversight committees of the Congress. Covert actions are considered when the National Security Council judges that U.S. foreign policy objectives may not be fully realized by normal diplomatic means and when military action is deemed too extreme an option. Therefore, the Agency may be directed to conduct a special activity abroad in support of foreign policy such that the role of the U.S. Government is neither apparent nor publicly acknowledged.

Does the Central Intelligence Agency participate in assassinations?

No. Presidential Executive Order No. 12333 explicitly prohibits the Central Intelligence Agency, either directly or indirectly, from engaging in assassinations. Internal safeguards and the Congressional oversight process assure compliance.

Does the Central Intelligence Agency engage in drug trafficking?

No. To the contrary, the Central Intelligence Agency assists the U.S. Government effort to thwart drug trafficking by providing intelligence information to the Department of Commerce, the Drug Enforcement Agency and the State Department.

What is the Central Intelligence Agency's role in combatting international terrorism?

The Central Intelligence Agency supports the overall United States Government effort to combat international terrorism by collecting, analyzing, and disseminating intelligence on foreign terrorist groups and individuals. It also conducts liaison with the intelligence and security services of friendly governments, shares counterterrorism intelligence information with and, on request, provides advice and training to these services. The Agency's counterterrorism specialists participate actively in developing strategies aimed at combatting terrorism and intelligence resources worldwide provide significant support to U.S. efforts to solve this grave problem.

How is the Central Intelligence Agency different from the KGB?

The Central Intelligence Agency and the KGB are very different because their missions and activities reflect the societies — one democratic and one totalitarian — of which they are a part. A major role of the KGB is internal security, including routine surveillance of Soviet citizens. The Agency has no law enforcement or security functions either at home or abroad. Unlike the Agency, which is governed by Presidential Executive Order and law, KGB activities are unrestrained. Moreover, the American people's elected officials oversee all U.S. intelligence activities through the Congressional Oversight process. The KGB answers to no one but the highest level officials of the Soviet party, who are not freely chosen by the Russian people.

Who works for the Central Intelligence Agency?

The Agency carefully selects well-qualified people in nearly all fields of study. Scientists, engineers, economists, linguists, mathematicians, secretaries, and computer specialists are but a few of the disciplines continually in demand. Some are specialists — physical and social scientists, doctors of medicine, lawyers, etc. — but many are generalists, people who have demonstrated their qualifications to hold the many varied positions that make up the bulk of the domestic and overseas staffs. Women, members of minority groups, and the handicapped are well represented in the ranks of the employed at the Central Intelligence Agency.

How many people work for the Central Intelligence Agency and what is its budget?

Neither the number of employees nor the size of the Agency's budget can be publicly disclosed. That knowledge would provide an advantage to our adversaries. While these subjects are classified, they are known in detail and scrutinized daily by the Office of Management and Budget and by the Intelligence Oversight and Appropriations Committees of both houses of the Congress. A common misconception is that the Agency has an unlimited budget, which is far from true. The resources allocated to intelligence are subject to the same rigorous examination and approval process as all other government organizations.

Does the Central Intelligence Agency give tours of its headquarters building in Langley, Virginia?

No. The idea was considered and tested but logistical problems and security considerations demonstrated it is just not possible.

Does the Central Intelligence Agency release publications to the public?

The Agency releases many unclassified publications in order to provide additional research aids to academic and business communities. The majority of these reports contain foreign or international economic and political information or are directories of foreign officials. They are readily available through most U.S. Government outlets. The Agency cannot, however, release many of its other reports because such studies are derived from sensitive sources.

William E. Colby was Director of the CIA from 1973 to 1976. After serving valiantly in OSS during World War II, he returned to Columbia Law School and obtained his degree, subsequently joining William Donovan's law firm. He joined CIA in 1950. After retiring from the agency, he reentered private law practice.

Q *What is the future of the Central Intelligence Agency?*

A The CIA in the future will focus more on accuracy of reporting and analysis and must strive for a better understanding of external groups. All in all, the agency's future is bright and I am optimistic.

Q *What about the technological area?*

A With new technology there will be fantastic changes—sensors, radar technology, new machines—all will help in creating more openness. Before, intelligence was collected to know what the adversary was doing; today it's the same, but the important difference is that with more openness, perhaps both sides will realize the other's intentions. The Soviets also with new technology will realize the United States does not wish to harm the USSR. The Soviets have 400 years of Russian history that demonstrates its adversaries have always invaded or desired the motherland's downfall.

Q *But what about covert action? Should we continue it?*

A Yes, but we must be careful. We must use it in situations where it is appropriate. It must be kept secret. It should not be moved to the military because the military's goal is to win in an all-out way. It should be retained in the CIA and used subtly, especially in the political arena. But again, it must be secret.

Q *Was the Yurchenko affair designed to embarrass the CIA?*

A No.

Q *Isn't one of the only ways to penetrate the CIA by an affair like Yurchenko?*

A You see, the CIA has probably never been penetrated at a high level due to excellent security in the agency. We must always assume that there could be a high-level penetration and be on guard, but the agency's security record is superb. Most of the other Western intelligence agencies have been penetrated many, many times—England, Germany, Holland, Norway, France, NATO, et cetera.

Q *What is the future of the war between the CIA and KGB?*

A It will continue to be the same.

Q *Will the KGB's goal for the 1990s be to plant more deep-cover agents in the United States?*

A No, it will be to obtain military secrets and focus on our technology.

Q *What are the strengths of the CIA today?*

A Technology, better analysis, and much better trained case officers.

Q *Has the media softened its criticism of the CIA*

A Yes, but it's a cyclical thing.

Q *How can the United States curtail operations against this country?*

A By legislation—agent identification procedures, so we know who works for foreign nations. By expulsions—find the spies and expel them from our country. By restrictions—restrict Soviet and East bloc intelligence officers from areas and topics of interest. Strengthen the FBI's counterintelligence.

Q *Can Americans run successful operations against the Soviets in Eastern Europe and the Soviet Union?*

A It's not easy, but we do it. There was a recent case of a high-level Soviet military officer working for us in Moscow.

Q *Many people believe the U.S. is great in technical collection and that this has supplanted the human role.*

A The technical area has supplemented, not replaced, the human agent. It has freed the human agent to concentrate on other, higher priorities. Technical collection has helped arms control by verifying, and in this nuclear age it's important for the entire world. Agents should be used for the intangibles—how political leaders think, how decisions are made, and what political forces are taking shape.

Q *Since the Church and Pike hearings into the conduct of the CIA, hasn't the agency suffered?*

A In some ways, yes. But the risks of oversight are necessary in our democracy, if they are reasonable. The Greenpeace affair and the Israeli case of spying against the U.S. are examples of poor oversight by France and Israel.

Q *Is it likely more third world nations will establish or expand their intelligence services?*

A Very definitely. But most espionage will be against their neighbors and will be regional and directly related to a nation's local interests. Only the United States and the Soviet Union have interests and resources to conduct intelligence gathering in a big way.

Q *Is the new kind of spy a Walter Mitty?*

A Yes. They are tawdry little people. They sell out their country for relatively small amounts of money. Before, spies in this country did it for ideological reasons. Now it's for money. Soviets and other Communists now coming over to us are doing it for ideological reasons. Recent defectors to the West are increasing and are likely to increase.

Q *What were your accomplishments? For what would you like to be remembered?*

A Getting us through the trauma of the investigations. Briefing senators who knew very little about the CIA. And trying to explain a secret organization without revealing the secrets. I attempted to explain and control an often reckless investigation. The abuses were few and far between. In operations, marrying technology to the clandestine services. I cannot discuss specific operations.

Q *What about the Glomar Explorer Project?*

A I can't discuss this.

Q *What about coordination with the intelligence community?*

A The CIA and DIA worked much better and so did the FBI and CIA during my administration.

Q *Should the CIA directorship be fixed for 10 years?*

A No. It should be subject to the President's choice.

Q *Who was the Best DCI?*

A It's hard to say just yet, perhaps John McCone. But I think Bill Casey may be a contender. McCone as an administrator and Bill Casey for reviving the CIA.

Center of CIA operations—Workers staff consoles in the operations center of the Central Intelligence Agency's headquarters at Langley, Virginia. The center acts as the central gathering point for data transmitted to CIA headquarters daily from agents stationed around the world.

Operations of the C.I.A.

Operations of the C.I.A.

David Atlee Phillips, regarded as a "superagent," was an operations officer for his entire career. For years Phillips operated in Latin America and the Caribbean. From agent to officer to chief-of-station to director of Latin American operations, Phillips performed functions in all aspects of operations including propaganda, collection, subversion, and managing intelligence officers and agents.

The Berlin Tunnel was a great CIA success. The CIA tapped into Soviet communications for more than 18 months. William King Harvey, fired from the FBI by J. Edgar Hoover, ran many operations like the Berlin Tunnel.

Inside CIA's Clandestine Service the DDO

The Directorate of Operations of the Central Intelligence Agency, known as the DDO, has been called "the secret CIA." The other CIA Directorates—Intelligence, Administration, and Science & Technology—produce classified estimates and analyses, perform quiet housekeeping duties, and develop secret designs and devices. The people who work in these directorates usually identify themselves to friends and neighbors as CIA employees.

But not DDO people. These CIA personnel engaged in secret duties overseas and their Washington headquarters are known as operatives in the Clandestine Service, also called the DDO (for its chief, the Deputy Director, Operations). They must lead double lives to work effectively abroad and, in some hostile areas, to survive. They must have a "cover" to conceal their espionage and covert action work. Their secret lives—they must hide the truth from neighbors, friends, even their doctors and bankers—must be maintained during Washington duty assignments so their cover will remain intact for subsequent overseas tours.

What the DDO Does

The Clandestine Service basically does two things: (1) it collects intelligence that will be processed by the Directorate of Intelligence into the estimates and analyses needed by policymakers to formulate policy, and (2) it undertakes programs to assist policymakers in carrying out a policy.

The first responsibility is called "espionage" and the second "covert action." Both involve the use of clandestine operations (the generic expression describes secret activities of whatever nature). Espionage seeks to uncover information important to the United States government which some foreign government or group wishes to keep secret. Covert action endeavors to persuade a foreign entity to take

137

Two new "ops" centers. The photo at the top shows an operations center which monitors cable traffic from CIA officers. The photo at bottom, another 24-hour "ops" center, coordinates intelligence from overt sources.

action or, in some cases, to refrain from an action. Circumstances and the nature of the persuasion preclude the attribution of covert action to the United States government. Propaganda in its many shades of gray (that is, degrees of concealment of sponsorship) may accomplish a covert action objective. Secret agents dealing with individuals in a position of influence are more likely to do so.

The primary DDO missions are espionage, or collecting intelligence, and counterespionage, or protecting its own secrets. The vast majority of the DDO's operations are concerned with the latter.

Oleg Penkovsky, recruited by the British and CIA, became a genuine defector who supplied important information to the West. Here he stands with a KGB guard over him at his trial. He was executed in 1963 for espionage.

How the DDO Collects Intelligence

DDO operatives overseas, usually called case officers, gather intelligence from spies who for one reason or another agree to reveal secrets belonging to their own government or group. Information collected from them is known as HUMINT, for human intelligence. DDO officers never refer to themselves—or to their counterparts in other intelligence agencies—as spies. They are intelligence officers; they are managers of spies. Spies become traitors for a variety of reasons, often for money. Some sell their country's secrets for other motives. Colonel Oleg Penkovsky, perhaps the most valuable spy ever to report to the West from Moscow, became an informant as a form of political protest against Soviet totalitarianism.

Vital overseas intelligence data is also gathered by technical means, such as eavesdropping on telephone calls, reading other peoples' mail, and establishing surveillance, sometimes photographic, on persons or places. Useful information is gleaned from listening devices, known as bugs, that infest offices and living quarters of government and political leaders. COMINT is intelligence gathered from communications or the activities that protect communications. SIGINT (signals) and ELINT (electronic) are associ-

ated with COMINT. The collection of outer space intelligence has already been dubbed by some as SPAINT.

In order to satisfy important customers in the White House, the Department of State, and the Pentagon, DDO officers must be prepared to perform unexpected tasks. A hypothetical example: The CIA is asked to report on the health of a foreign leader. An attempt to obtain the information from the foreign leader's physician fails. At that point, would the case officer be asked to obtain, without the foreign leader's knowledge, a specimen of his urine?

The best DDO intelligence is that which is provided by one source and then is confirmed by other sources.

The CIA used human *and* technical sources to achieve the greatest espionage coup in U.S. history. In 1962 the Soviet Union began to secretly construct offensive missile sites in Cuba, only 90 miles from Florida. The DDO learned from its human sources in Cuba that huge elongated objects had arrived from Russia. Then an agent reported the location of new military construction. These two HUMINT reports were augmented by technical collection when CIA's photographic intelligence plane, the famous U-2, photographed the construction, enabling CIA photo-

Labels on image: VANS, PROB FIRECAN RADAR, FROG, 9 AMPHIB ARMORED RECON VEHICLES, 5 BM-13 ROCKET LAUNCHERS, MISSILE TRANSPORTER, 2 TANK RECOVERY, 11 T-54 TANKS, 9 SU-100, B TR-40, 5 POSS B TR-50

MILITARY CAMPS, REMEDIOS AREA, CUBA   **25 OCTOBER 1962**

This photo shows the accelerated contruction of offensive missiles in Cuba. Constant U-2 overflights as well as "human" agents supplied the U.S. with hard facts of Soviet moves in Cuba.

interpreters to identify the missiles. CIA Director John McCone then warned John F. Kennedy of the Soviet threat, telling the President precisely what the capabilities of the Russian missiles were—coincidentally, Oleg Penkovsky had provided the manuals for that particular missile system!

Covert Action— The DDO's Unique Responsibility

While the Clandestine Service officer is primarily concerned with espionage and counterespionage, some clandestine operations are carried out with the objective of changing situations or influencing developments overseas. That process is called covert action. The popular definition of covert action has become the option a U.S. President has in foreign crisis developments between an ineffective diplomatic protest on the one hand and, on the other, sending in the Marines.

Covert action operations are controversial. Some have resulted in sensational headlines and several Congressional investigations, the most thorough being the Senate inquiry in 1975-1976, known for its chairman as the Church Committee. The scrutiny was intense, ranging from failed assassination attempts against Fidel Castro to CIA operations in Chile. The DDO was damaged, some say crippled, for several years following the Church Committee investigation.

Covert action is a unique responsibility for CIA—no other agency is authorized to conduct peacetime covert action. "A dubious honor," grumble some DDO officers.

There is nothing new about covert action. It can be traced as far back as the military and political musings of the Chinese general Sun Tzu in 500 B.C. through Machiavelli, who concluded in the 16th century that there were only two ways to overcome an enemy: by force or by fraud. During World War II covert action

LAUNCH PAD WITH ERECTOR

CHERRY PICKER

LAUNCH PAD WITH ERECTOR

MISSILE READY BLDGS

OXIDIZER VEHICLES

FUELING VEHICLES

MEDIUM RANGE BALLISTIC MISSILE BASE IN CUBA

Photos like this one were brought to President Kennedy. They showed Soviet missiles.

was a weapon in the cloak-and-dagger arsenal of General William Donovan's Office of Strategic Services.

When the CIA was created in 1947 it was not foreseen that the agency would engage in covert action. But the charter which authorized the CIA contained an instruction that the agency should "perform such other functions and duties related to intelligence affecting the national security." The elasticity of that phrase was tested when the first DCI, Admiral Roscoe Hillenkoetter, was asked by senior officials of the Truman administration if the "other such functions and duties" included covert action. Hillenkoetter asked CIA's chief lawyer, Lawrence R. Houston, if the phrase did provide authority. Houston said no. Requested to review the matter, Houston returned with the opinion that CIA could legitimately

conduct covert action *if* the President, as commander in chief, arranged for a special directive authorizing such activity, and *if* the Congress appropriated the necessary funds.

That was the beginning of the systematic use of covert action by the U.S. in its Cold War conflict with the Soviet Union. During his two administrations operations were authorized by President Dwight D. Eisenhower on the recommendations of his secretary of state, John Foster Dulles, and implemented by Dulles's brother, Allen Welsh Dulles. John Foster Dulles was an ardent Cold Warrior committed to thwarting Soviet expansion. He approached the edge of confrontation with the Russians so frequently that his foreign policy became known as "brinkmanship." When he decided to augment his overt programs with covert action he had only to turn to this brother. The

141

President Fidel Castro has been the nemesis of the CIA for more than 25 years. Almost all CIA operations against Castro have failed.

younger Dulles had conducted a dazzling array of secret operations in Europe for the OSS during World War II. Before becoming DCI he had served briefly as chief of the DDO (known then as DDI), and he was always eager to engage the Russian adversary in the dark alleys of the world. It was a cozy sibling relationship.

The Dulles brothers lacked the authority to conduct major covert action abroad on their own, but they were encouraged to do so by President Eisenhower. Only in recent years have historians discovered that Eisenhower was an enthusiastic advocate of clandestine political and paramilitary activities. He had not forgotten how effectively intelligence operations,

frequently involving psychological warfare and guerrilla sabotage, had served him when he was the supreme commander of Allied forces during World War II. One historian began to write a biography of Eisenhower 10 years after he left office believing the former general had become a pacifist in the White House. The historian wrote several years later: "But research into Eisenhower's previously classified papers highlighted for me . . . the pivotal role played by covert operations, secrecy, dirty tricks, and counterinsurgency . . . ."

Whether our country should or should not conduct covert action is often debated. But most chiefs of state have not hesitated to use it.

The epitome of the operations man—007, James Bond (as portrayed by actor Sean Connery). The indestructable British agent is the creation of Ian Fleming. Most of the "gimmicks" Fleming created were from actual CIA pieces of tradecraft developed for the CIA operations branch.

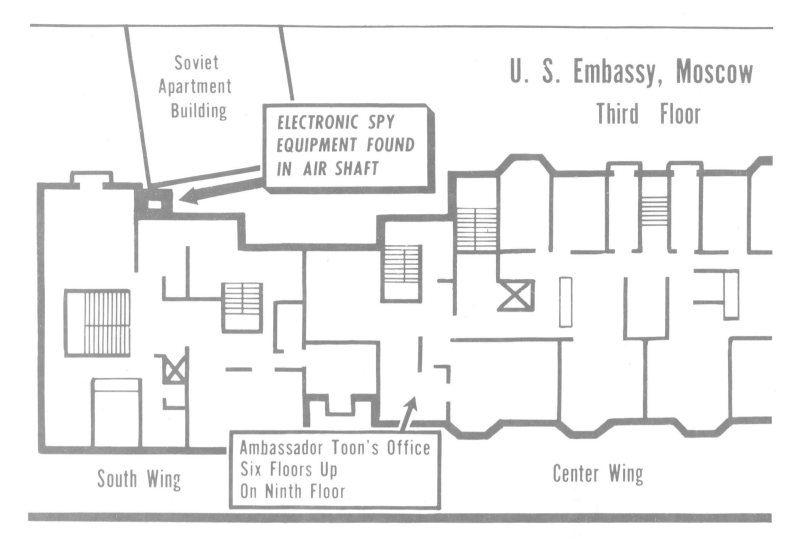

Soviet Apartment Building

ELECTRONIC SPY EQUIPMENT FOUND IN AIR SHAFT

U. S. Embassy, Moscow
Third Floor

Ambassador Toon's Office Six Floors Up On Ninth Floor

South Wing

Center Wing

KGB operations against the U.S. have been increasingly in the electronic area. Soviet "ops" personnel planted electronic surveillance equipment in an air shaft of the U.S. embassy in Moscow. The diagram shows the location of the air shaft and nearby Soviet apartment building where a tunnel led from a surveillance room to the air shaft. CIA security personnel discovered the bug.

Counterintelligence—
Protecting the CIA's Family Jewels

Counterintelligence is often thought of as an activity separate and apart from intelligence collection. Actually it is the same thing. The difference is that the information is gathered not to assist policymakers, but so that CIA will be warned of hostile attempts to weaken or destroy the agency. CI operations, as they are called, are primarily concerned with uncovering hostile penetrations. A human penetration, popularly known as a "mole," is one method used to discover the secrets of an adversary intelligence service. Among other things a penetration can be a listening device or an operation that deciphers encoded messages.

While the British, French, Russian, and other intelligence services have been repeatedly penetrated, the CIA has a good record of protecting its secrets from enemies. The record is spotty, however, when it comes to keeping secrets from American journalists.

In addition to espionage and counterespionage, DDO officers abroad have a variety of responsibilities. Some of the tasks are performed daily and are almost humdrum in nature. When carrying out these chores intelligence officers complain that the symbol for their work should be changed from a cloak and dagger to a computer and a private detective's badge. Other DDO tasks overseas are complicated, sometimes perilous and, on occasion, charged with the excitement of James Bond-like adventures.

The trickiest assignment for a DDO officer abroad is when he or she uses nonofficial or "deep" cover. Some DDO officers enjoy official cover as employees of some official United States establishment. If they find themselves in trouble because of unprofessional conduct or bad luck they are protected by official passports. At worst, they are declared *persona non grata* and sent home.

Kim Philby, a British intelligence officer, was actually a Soviet spy for more than 20 years. Philby has been the subject of more articles and books than any other operations man (excluding the fictitious James Bond). Here Philby is shown in 1955 after being cleared by Harold Macmillan of being the "third man" inside the British Secret Service, the others being Guy Burgess and Donald Maclean. Philby was finally exposed by CIA man William King Harvey.

The high comedy of electronic spying probably came when it was discovered that the Great Seal of the United States in the embassy in Moscow was bugged. Here U.N. Ambassador Henry Cabot Lodge shows to everyone's obvious pleasure the electronic device. Soviet Ambassador Andrei Gromyko, at the far left, is also enjoying it. Both the Soviet KGB and the CIA have extensive electronic eavesdropping and security staffs. These operations have increased on both sides. Measures and countermeasures are taken constantly as new technology is advanced to conceal, bug, debug, and listen from far away. Now all top secret areas—the White House, CIA, military intelligence, and so forth—are lead-lined.

The deep-cover DDO officer has no such protection. If he or she is in trouble they are subject to prosecution under local laws. The American government cannot come to their aid—such an approach by a U.S. embassy would confirm the fact that the American was, in fact, a DDO operative.

In some situations Clandestine Service personnel overseas must react to unusual and unanticipated developments that call for rapid decision-making and impeccable "tradecraft," the careful conduct of intelligence chores in such a manner that errors and sloppy performance do not come back to haunt them or result in disaster (in intelligence parlance, a "flap"). Here are three examples of DDO overseas case officer activity, all having actually occurred in Latin America.

It was learned at a CIA station that a meeting was about to occur between a Soviet KGB officer from the local embassy and a indigenous KGB spy. It was decided to "intercept" the encounter. A CIA officer posed as a Russian to meet the local agent and learn from him details about the relations between the Soviet embassy and the agent's political party. The CIA man approached the agent, explaining in Russian that his regular KGB contact was ill. To make the scenario realistic, another CIA case officer who spoke Russian played the role of the ubiquitous Russian chauffeur, waiting behind the wheel of a nearby car. There was an exchange of money, documents, and a long conversation. When it was over the agent said to the CIA officer: "I've been working for the KGB for six years, and you are the most professional KGB officer I've ever met!"

In another Latin American country it was necessary for a four-person CIA team of case officers to make a surreptitious entry, a break-in, to gain access to the offices of a hostile foreign country. It was decided that members of the team must pose as electricians. This posed a problem as one of the CIA case officers was a woman—and there are no women electricians in Latin America. So, the CIA woman was disguised as a man, complete with a bushy mustache!

In 1975 George Matthews of the British Communist party shows a listening device and the piece of woodwork in which it was installed. Both the CIA and the British Secret Service got the blame. The device was discovered during remodeling in 1975, but even Mr. Matthews thought the "bug" was installed in 1948, the last time the building was remodeled. The device consists of a small battery with a metal case. The battery was still working when the device was discovered.

The Soviet newspaper *Izvestia* in 1980 claimed that two U.S. diplomats who were actually CIA officers planted this fake tree stump near a Soviet military installation. The stump supposedly contained an electronic spying apparatus. *Izvestia* gave no date for the incident, only the names of the diplomats—Weatherbee and Corbin.

Salvador Allende before he was overthrown. Although initially thought to be a CIA operation, recent evidence suggests that the CIA was not involved.

Three Major Covert Action Successes
(From a President's Viewpoint)

In 1953 President Eisenhower approved a CIA operation to remove from power in Iran an erratic prime minister named Mossadegh, who threatened American and British interests despite the fact that the young Shah was pro-American. During a period of rioting a CIA officer named Kermit Roosevelt, his DDO case officers, and their Iranian agents used nerve, guile, and a bag of money to start the beginning of the end. They *organized* the riots. Paid protesters, with huge Iranian weightlifters in the vanguard, took control of the pandemonium, shaped it into a political action event, and installed a new prime minister. Mossadegh fled and the Shah returned to the throne. President Eisenhower thought the entire operation was dandy.

In 1954 President Eisenhower became concerned with growing Soviet influence in Latin America, particularly in Guatemala. A CIA covert action operation ensued. It was largely a make-believe scenario of propaganda and psychological warfare; but it succeeded in making the president of the country believe he was about to be overthrown. He suddenly resigned and sought asylum in the Mexican embassy along with several hundred of his advisors (one of them a young Argentine named Che Guevara). At a subsequent White House meeting President Eisenhower turned to Allen Dulles, saying, "Thank you, Allen. You have averted a Soviet beachhead in Central America."

Throughout the decade of the 1960s the CIA played a major role in preventing Fidel Castro's effort to export his revolution by moving Cuban troops into Latin America, Africa, and the Middle East. Primarily because of that CIA program Castro failed everywhere, from the Congo to Bolivia. Presidents Kennedy, Johnson, and Ford were pleased by the work done for them by DCIs John McCone, Admiral William Raborn, and Richard Helms.

149

The CIA has no monopoly on dirty tricks. In the United States, however, the public chafes at such behavior in peacetime. The KGB helps publicize anything that could be construed as anti-CIA.

YOU SHOULD KNOW BETTER NOT TO GET INVOLVED IN DIRTY TRICKS !!

Three Major Covert Action Failures

President Eisenhower did not approve, nor did John Foster Dulles, in 1956 when in Indonesia a feisty president named Sukarno became increasingly powerful and authoritarian after instituting a policy he called "guided democracy." Sukarno drifted toward the political left, established relations with Communists at home and abroad. A major CIA covert action took place into 1957 when the agency supported a group of dissident colonels. The operation was the first major DDO covert action failure, collapsing after an American pilot was shot down and imprisoned by Sukarno. But CIA was not criticized by the press or by Congress—the covert action failure was a *secret* failure.

There was little secret in 1961 about the Bay of Pigs, the worst covert action fiasco in CIA's history. Approved by President Eisenhower and carried out under President Kennedy, the original plan called for the training of about 100 Cubans who were to return to Cuban mountains *carrying their own weapons.* That

plan was discarded in favor of a major military endeavor calling for a brigade of 1,400 men *and a platoon of tanks!* The operation turned into a disaster after President Kennedy decided for political reasons that he must cancel plans to provide air cover for the invasion force.

In 1970 the DDO suffered a major defeat when an attempt to block the inauguration of Marxist President Salvador Allende in Chile failed. The idea of overthrowing the Chilean leader was President Richard Nixon's—he had summoned DCI Richard Helms and surprised him with the order to conduct the covert action. The failure extended into the public relations area in 1973. Allende was overthrown by the Chilean military, and he died in the attack on the capitol building in Santiago. Despite the conclusion of the Church Committee that the CIA was not responsible for that 1973 coup, most people in the world are convinced that CIA did overthrow Allende—and many Americans believe it as well.

The truly significant technology of the U-2 was the clear, detailed photos that U.S. and CIA-sponsored technology gave. It aided operations agents and helped direct agents in gathering other information that the U-2 could now pick up.

Here a CIA photo analyst interprets a high resolution posturization of an area.

A CIA model maker develops a scale model of an area.

152

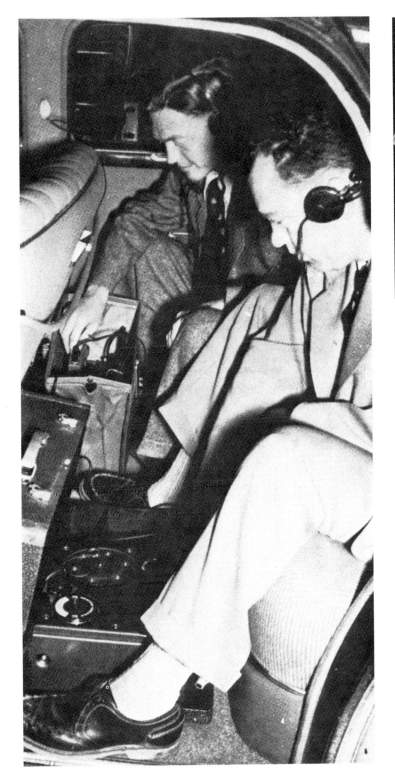

Two CIA men with a mobile bugging operation. This photo, taken in the early 1950s, shows an early type of eavesdropping.

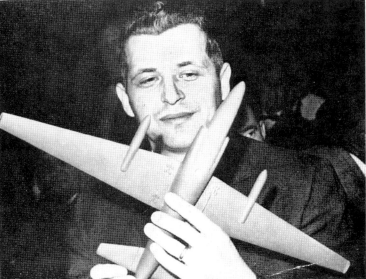

Gary Powers and a model of the plane he piloted when shot down over the Soviet Union.

Paramilitary Operations— A Special Kind of Covert Action

The Pigs fiasco marked the end of highly visible Cold War confrontations between American and Soviet interests. But while it cooled down, the Cold War was not over.

Sometimes CIA covert action has taken the form of support to local "secret armies," as in Laos during the period when U.S. troops were fighting in neighboring Vietnam. Such a paramilitary operation can be a "secret war" from the vantage point of the clandestine operator. While wars cannot be secret, CIA involvement in them can be—though in recent years there has been little evidence to sustain that conviction. In Central America, for instance, the Reagan administration's "secret army" of Nicaraguan *contras* has been constantly in the headlines.

Despite the controversy about covert action there is little indication that American presidents will not continue to employ it through the CIA so long as the conflict with the Soviet Union continues.

Thus it is unlikely that in the future the CIA will not maintain a Clandestine Service to collect intelligence most of the time, and to conduct covert action some of the time.

A listing of CIA operations would have to include propaganda and support of political parties, Guatemala, Cuba, Vietnam, Africa, Santo Domingo, and so forth. However, there is one operation that the CIA hopes is not counted: In the early 1980s the British, French, and Americans planned to topple Colonel Muammer el-Qaddafi. The CIA pulled out of the operation and demanded it not proceed.

WANTED RECHERCHÉ

ILICH RAMIREZ- SANCHEZ - FPS 827669A

ALIASES: "CARLOS", CLARKE, CENON MARIA (20-6-45 - N.Y., USA); GEBHARD, GLEN (1-8-50 - N.Y., USA); MARTINEZ-TORRES, CARLOS ANDRES (4-5-47 - BOLTERO, PERU); EUSEPI, MASSIMO (24-1-48, BELLEGRA, ITALY); MULLER-BERNAL, ADOLFO JOSE (CHILEAN NATIONALITY).

BORN: 12 OCT., 1949	NE: 12 OCTOBRE 1949
P. O. B.: VENEZUELA	LIEU DE NAISSANCE: VENEZUELA
HEIGHT: 5'9"	TAILLE: 5'9"
HAIR: CURLY, THICK, BROWN, SHORT	CHEVEUX: BOUCLES, ABONDANTS, BRUNS ET COURTS
BUILD: FAIRLY HEAVY	CORPULENCE: ASSEZ FORTE
SPEAKS SPANISH, ARABIC, RUSSIAN	PARLE: L'ESPAGNOL, L'ARABE ET LE RUSSE
HOLDS VENEZUELAN PASSPORT NO. 498056	DETIENT UN PASSEPORT VENEZUELIEN NO 498056

WARRANT FOR THE ARREST OF THE ABOVE-NAMED IS HELD BY THE REGIONAL COURT, VIENNA, AUSTRIA, FOR STRONG SUSPICION OF PARTIALLY COMMITTED PARTIALLY ATTEMPTED MURDER EXTORSIONATE KIDNAPPING AND TRESPASSING.

ALSO WANTED BY FRENCH AUTHORITIES FOR LOCATION.

EXTREMELY DANGEROUS AND WILL NOT HESITATE TO OPEN FIRE.

IF LOCATED ARREST AND ADVISE THE COMMISSIONER RCMP, OTTAWA, ONT.

UN MANDAT POUR L'ARRESTATION DU SUSNOMME EST DETENU PAR LA COUR REGIONALE DE VIENNE, AUTRICHE, OU IL EST FORTEMENT SOUPCONNE DE TENTATIVE ET DE COMMISSION PARTIELLES DE MEURTRE, D'ENLEVEMENT AVEC EXTORSION ET D'INTRUSION.

AUSSI RECHERCHE PAR LES AUTORITES FRANCAISES EN VUE DE DECOUVRIR SON LIEU DE REFUGE.

EXTREMEMENT DANGEREUX ET N'HESITERAIT PAS A FAIRE USAGE DE SES ARMES.

SI DÉPISTÉ, ARRÊTER ET EN INFORMER LE COMMISSAIRE, GRC, OTTAWA, ONT.

DANGEROUS   DANGEREUX

SPECIAL WANTED CIRCULAR
NO. 247 - APRIL 29, 1976
RCMP IDENTIFICATION SERVICES

CIRCULAIRE SPÉCIALE DE PERSONNES
RECHERCHÉES NO 247, LE 29 AVRIL 1976
SERVICES DE L'IDENTITE DE LA G.R.C.

Almost all of the stars on the memorial are in honor of operations men killed in the line of duty.

David Atlee Phillips served in the CIA for 25 years, rising to become head of operations for all of Latin America. In 1975, he founded the Association of Former Intelligence Officers (AFIO). He lectures frequently and is currently writing his fifth book on intelligence.

Q *How does a typical operation begin? Is a decision made at CIA headquarters? Is it made in the field? What's the process of getting an operation going?*

A Operations begin for a number of reasons. By far the greatest number begins to fill a requirement, a requirement which is posed by a U.S. President or Secretary of State or perhaps an American ambassador in the field.

Q *But it has to come from that high up?*

A It depends on the type of requirement. Small operations which fit into a generally approved program—such as, we try to inhibit the flow of hard drugs into this country, we try to learn what we can about foreign, hostile intelligence services—those things often initiate within the framework of general approval within the CIA itself. Larger operations of the kind that we read about in history books originate because a President or Secretary of State or perhaps an American ambassador says it's about time we did this.

Q *Would you define operations?*

A Operations is a part of clandestine operations, which is the generic name for secret activities of whatever kind. There is covert action of which the Bay of Pigs, though a failure, is one example. But the vast majority of operations concern attempts to recruit people to provide information, attempts to protect your own establishment from penetration by foreign powers, meeting the requirements laid on by political leaders and military leaders and answering a whole myriad of questions. Much of the intelligence that is gathered is useless because it's overtaken by events. But it's gathered just in case it's needed.

Q *It's a paper that you can't subscribe to?*

A That you can't subscribe to, an extremely limited list of readers that it goes to in the intelligence community and in the government.

Q *Operations is not just a CIA activity. It's part of any intelligence gathering agency—*

A With the exception of covert action. Covert action is the dubious honor of the CIA. In peacetime, it's the only agency authorized to conduct covert action. In wartime, anything goes with anyone.

Q *Of all the clandestine agencies in the world, which is the most aggressive in terms of operations?*

A In terms of operations, the most aggressive and certainly the best in that field is the Israeli service, the Mossad. We remember such coups as the raid on Entebbe, when they got their people back from a hijacking situation in Africa. And they are very, very good, and one of the reasons is obviously because they feel they need to be good, they need to be tough as a matter of national survival. The British, from the operational standpoint, must be given the worst of marks because of the bad luck they've had in being penetrated by moles. Nevertheless, the British are very, very good at economic intelligence, which is very important in some countries. The Soviets have a pretty good intelligence service, one of the four best in the world. There are more people who work for the KGB—and that's only one of the Soviet services—than all the rest of the intelligence services of the world combined. The American CIA, I think, ranks up until the mid-1970s as probably the best intelligence service in the world. Certainly even now it has the best history of protecting itself from hostile penetrations. Despite all of the stories we've seen recently, they're relatively low-level penetrations, not of the Philby type. Coming up fast is the Cuban intelligence service, which is almost 25 years old and has improved dramatically from the days when their operatives were the laughing stock of the diplomatic community abroad. They would always show up at diplomatic parties with .45 pistols stuck in their back pockets.

Q *Could you trace the intelligence process from the time the information is gathered?*

A In professional parlance, there's a procedure known as the intelligence cycle. And it begins with the acquisition of information. And that is done either through technical means, ranging from small, black boxes to high-altitude cameras, or the use of human agents. In this cycle, there are two important things that are involved. You want to know about intentions and about capabilities. Those are the two things any intelligence operation involves if you're trying to get information. Capabilities—how many missiles does the Soviet Union have? Intentions—does someone plan to use them? Everything boils down to those two things. In the field overseas, it is usually shaped into some sort of meaningful form—that is, if it's related to other information that's come before— by a person known as a reports officer. The reports officer prepares the material, which is then sent to Washington. In Washington, the intelligence cycle involves the dissemination of this information to all professionals who might be able to contribute something to the final product. And these primarily include analysts, the experts in their areas—their geographical area or their subject area—who can take this information and refine it even further. The next step is the distribution of this material to the customers, who may be military— the Pentagon—or political—the White House or the National Security Council. It can be terribly, terribly urgent and it's a matter of possible war, say, or something like that. It means that the President is awakened in the middle of the night by a CIA Director who is knocking on the front door of the White House. Or it may take the form of distribution in a CIA publication, like the *National Intelligence Daily*, which is just a small newspaper, but all the stories are secret and all or most of the photographs are unusual.

Q *You said that the CIA performed better before the 1970s.*

A Yes. Right after the troubles that the intelligence communty went through in the mid-seventies, there were eight oversight committees in Congress. That didn't work; too many people involved. Now there are two, one in each house, and that is more manageable. Even now, though, there are problems of leaks, and

the leaks seem to come from the Congress, from the White House, and from the intelligence services themselves. People seem to find political reasons to have the leaks. That's the reason the CIA cannot possibly be as good as it once was. This situation of constant revelation of secrets and of operations has meant, first, that allies are hesitant to work with the CIA; next, agents and potential agents hesitate to work for the CIA because they have fears that their identities will be revealed; third, American officials who are working within the CIA are bound to have their problems of morale when they work hard on an operation and from their standpoint it succeeds, only to become publicized, which means that suddenly there's a failure on the clandestine side.

Q *Would you cite an example of an operation from your own experience, one that you were involved in?*

A Alright. One operation I was involved in concerned the handling of a defector. People are generally surprised when you tell them that of defectors, the majority of them sooner or later return to their country. Remember the famous case a short while ago of Stalin's daugher. And more recently Yurchenko.

In Mexico City in the early 1960s, a defector from the DGI, the Cuban Directorate General of Intelligence, walked into the American embassy, where I was then stationed. Another officer and I were given the job, once it was established that he was an authentic Cuban intelligence officer, of handling this case. And so we sat up all night talking to this man, asking him questions. It was very important because he was the first defector from the Cuban intelligence service, a fledgling service we didn't know much about. But during the evening I remembered the words my boss told me when I went out to meet this defector: Remember that a defector is a person who has just committed emotional suicide and must be handled very carefully. Remembering that advice, I decided that the proper way to handle this defector was to get him out of Mexico City and into the United States on the first available plane. That was early in the morning, and so another officer and I went with this man in a car toward the airport to catch that plane. Suddenly, in the middle of Mexico City, he shouted, I can't do it, I can't do it, and he jumped out of our car and ran away down the street and ran back to the Cuban embassy. He was in that embassy

and was preparing to return to Cuba, but he had no clothes or luggage. We had his luggage because he brought it with him when he defected. We managed to get a message to him in some new luggage the embassy sent for; we knew that it must be for him. The note said, Why are you doing this? You will not live if you go back to Cuba. You really shouldn't take this chance. When you get to the airport, you once again will have a chance to defect. Well, a couple of days later, he was escorted to the airport by the Cuban ambassador and the Cuban chief of station. And I was standing there when he walked in, and he looked up at me and recognized me, and he just shook his head and went out and got on that plane to Cuba. Two weeks later, his death was announced in the Cuban newspaper. He had been on the scene, the newspaper said, of a gunfight between policemen and bank robbers and had been so unlucky that he had been shot through the head and killed. I suspected then and I strongly suspect now that it wasn't bad luck at all, but simply the execution of a traitor. So there is an example of an operation that was a failure because he didn't remain a defector. Yet in that one night, we learned more about the Cuban intelligence service than we had known all the time before.

We talk about operations and the ways that we get information and the way we recruit spies and defectors and counter-defectors, and covert action—we talk about that because that's the James Bond side of the business, the glamorous side. The truth is, however, that the great majority of intelligence work is overt, and the majority of the people who work in intelligence are people who can say that they work at the CIA, for instance. Well, what do you do at the CIA? I'm a Soviet weapons analyst, or I'm an expert on Africa, or I'm an expert on agriculture. There's no secret about these people or the people who clean out the building or prepare the food in the cafeteria. So the man who drives into CIA headquarters in a bright red car looking like James Bond might very well be one of the CIA barbers. One cannot be sure.

The Intelligence Community

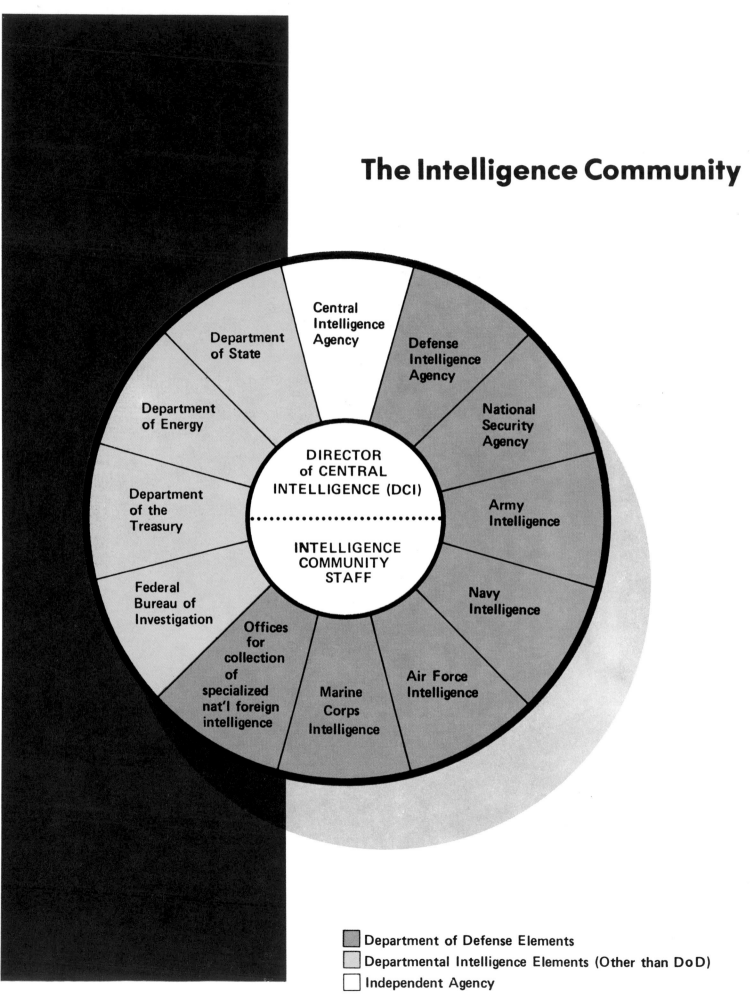

Central Intelligence Agency

Department of State

Department of Energy

Department of the Treasury

Federal Bureau of Investigation

Offices for collection of specialized nat'l foreign intelligence

Defense Intelligence Agency

National Security Agency

Army Intelligence

Navy Intelligence

Air Force Intelligence

Marine Corps Intelligence

DIRECTOR of CENTRAL INTELLIGENCE (DCI)

INTELLIGENCE COMMUNITY STAFF

Department of Defense Elements

Departmental Intelligence Elements (Other than DoD)

Independent Agency

Intelligence Community

Intelligence Community

The Director of Central Intelligence (DCI) is responsible for coordinating the intelligence from all the departments which, together, form the intelligence community.

The DCI is chief advisor to the President and the National Security Council on all matters relating to national security. He is head of the central intelligence and of all other departments inside the intelligence community.

The Defense Intelligence Agency

The Defense Intelligence Agency provides foreign intelligence and counterintelligence for the Secretary of Defense, the Joint Chiefs of Staff, the Unified and Specific Commands, and other authorized agencies.

All military intelligence services are directly responsible to this agency. Each of the four services has its intelligence arm and each has its own intelligence requirements. The DIA coordinates all their contributions.

Among the responsibilities of the DIA is the assignment of military attachés to U.S. embassies throughout the world. The defense attachés—senior officers from any of the four services—are military diplomats. While they do not engage in any illegal

An aerial view of CIA headquarters, Langley, Virginia.

acts, their chief objective is to discover as much detailed information as they can about the military establishments of their new countries of residence. They conduct liaison with local military units and collect battle order information on foreign armies.

Their role becomes more clearly defined in times of war, or in sufficiently volatile peacetime situations. Military attachés then drop their passive role-playing and become actively engaged in covert intelligence activities.

Attachés from all countries prefer to minimize their activities in intelligence, but their covert activities are widely known. It is commonly accepted, for instance, that the Soviet Union's military intelligence generally uses attaché cover for its agents.

The supersecret National Security Agency is often confused with the National Security Council and thought to be part of army intelligence. It is the most secret of all U.S. intelligence agencies for the reason that over the years, many intelligence breakthroughs have been made not by human agents, but by breaking codes and ciphers. The NSA develops and is responsible for the security of American cable traffic, ciphers, and codes, and it also intercepts and attempts to break others' codes and ciphers. The NSA also helped develop some of the first computers, and it employs top American scientists in mathematics, physics, languages, and "thinking skills." The NSA maintains listening stations around the world and is probably a more important target for Soviet espionage than the CIA.

NSA

Of all the secret organizations, least is known about the National Security Agency, yet it is one of the most powerful. It has full responsibility for all U.S. communications security activities and for development of foreign intelligence information.

The agency's research and development program has made many significant advances in the field of specialized communications equipment. Some of these have represented significant breakthroughs in the commercial world at large as well as the specialized fields of security and intelligence.

The NSA's laboratories near Baltimore, Maryland, produced the first large-scale computer as well as the first solid-state computer; its data processing and computing center is one of the largest in the world.

Cryptography—the development of codes and ciphers—is a major function of the NSA, and increasingly sophisticated cryptographic systems are being scientifically devised and tested for the transmission of sensitive intelligence.

NSA's secret activities in the field of foreign intelligence include the collection, processing, and dissemination of signals intelligence to the President and other authorized government policymakers, including the military services. It also processes information for counterintelligence purposes, provides signals intelligence support for military operations, and conducts foreign cryptographical liaison relationships for intelligence purposes.

In the area of foreign intelligence, the NSA abides by the policies formulated by the Director of Central Intelligence.

Although it works in close collaboration with the CIA, it is an agency of the Department of Defense.

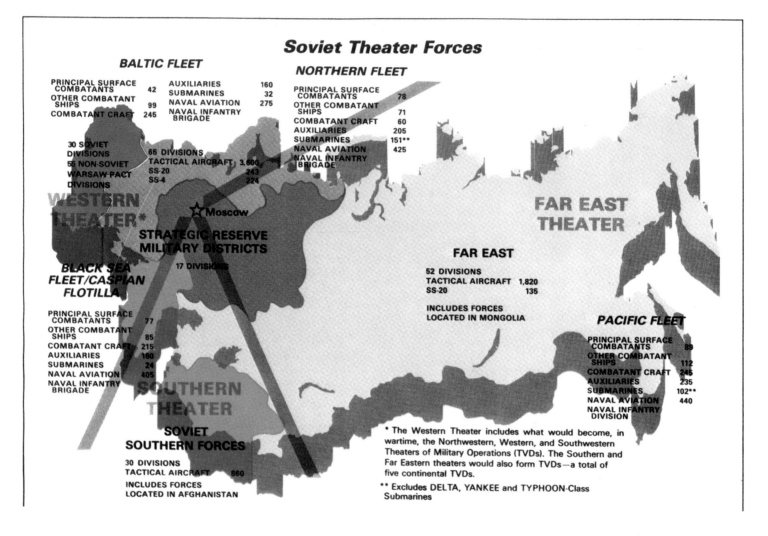

Soviet Theater Forces

BALTIC FLEET

PRINCIPAL SURFACE COMBATANTS	42	AUXILIARIES	160
OTHER COMBATANT SHIPS	99	SUBMARINES	32
		NAVAL AVIATION	275
COMBATANT CRAFT	245	NAVAL INFANTRY BRIGADE	

NORTHERN FLEET

PRINCIPAL SURFACE COMBATANTS	78
OTHER COMBATANT SHIPS	71
COMBATANT CRAFT	60
AUXILIARIES	205
SUBMARINES	151**
NAVAL AVIATION	425
NAVAL INFANTRY BRIGADE	

WESTERN THEATER*

30 SOVIET DIVISIONS	
55 NON-SOVIET WARSAW PACT DIVISIONS	
65 DIVISIONS	
TACTICAL AIRCRAFT	3,600
SS-20	243
SS-4	224

★ Moscow

STRATEGIC RESERVE MILITARY DISTRICTS

17 DIVISIONS

FAR EAST THEATER

FAR EAST

52 DIVISIONS	
TACTICAL AIRCRAFT	1,820
SS-20	135

INCLUDES FORCES LOCATED IN MONGOLIA

BLACK SEA FLEET/CASPIAN FLOTILLA

PRINCIPAL SURFACE COMBATANTS	77
OTHER COMBATANT SHIPS	85
COMBATANT CRAFT	215
AUXILIARIES	180
SUBMARINES	24
NAVAL AVIATION	405
NAVAL INFANTRY BRIGADE	

SOUTHERN THEATER

SOVIET SOUTHERN FORCES

30 DIVISIONS	
TACTICAL AIRCRAFT	860

INCLUDES FORCES LOCATED IN AFGHANISTAN

PACIFIC FLEET

PRINCIPAL SURFACE COMBATANTS	89
OTHER COMBATANT SHIPS	112
COMBATANT CRAFT	245
AUXILIARIES	235
SUBMARINES	102**
NAVAL AVIATION	440
NAVAL INFANTRY DIVISION	

* The Western Theater includes what would become, in wartime, the Northwestern, Western, and Southwestern Theaters of Military Operations (TVDs). The Southern and Far Eastern theaters would also form TVDs—a total of five continental TVDs.

** Excludes DELTA, YANKEE and TYPHOON-Class Submarines

Army intelligence—always the largest branch in the services as far as manpower is concerned—involves more than 42,000 people. This map showing Soviet forces was gathered, verified, and analyzed by all the service branches. Army intelligence was responsible for the Soviet army portion. Attachés worldwide gathered the intelligence. Changes in troop movements, additions to the numbers of troops, and any command changes are top priority to army intelligence, which constantly supplies the CIA and U.S. forces with updated information.

Army Intelligence

Over 40,000 personnel are employed by the U.S. Army Intelligence service. While technology relating to satellites and cryptology are more the province of the air force and navy, the army's intelligence gathering prioritizes military resources and strength of arms.

The army collects information about Soviet technological abilities and advances, but even more important is intelligence about troop dispositions, numbers of tanks, and movement and rotation of troops. Satellite information and the codebreaking conducted by various defense agencies help the army in planning strategy.

The Soviet army and its allies are larger than the U.S. Army and rely heavily on the tank. Blitzkrieg warfare, overwhelming strength, and support by Russian paratroop and rocket forces present a formidable conventional adversary. Monitoring the Soviet army is of paramount importance to the U.S. army, and its activities include gathering intelligence about Soviet equipment—tanks, trucks, supply lines, small arms, artillery, the development of new arms—as well as personal intelligence about the various Soviet commanders: how they think, their habits, and the forces at their command.

DEFENSE INTELLIGENCE AGENCY

TO: CIA

FROM: DIA, Soviet Desk, personnel analysis

Subject: **V.F. Tolubko**
Deputy Minister of Defense, Commander-in-Chief Rocket Forces

Subject has just returned from Warsaw Pact maneuvers in East Germany. Subject was accompanied by Y.F. Ivanovsky, Commander-in-Chief Ground Forces. Subject spent seven days observing and directing two divisions of Soviet Rocket Forces. Tolubko has been responsible for developing and building up his forces. During maneuvers Tolubko stressed an increase in forces due to what he believes is aggressive buildup of NATO forces in missiles.

Tolubko was involved in a heated argument with his superior S.F. Akhromeyev over posture of his forces during maneuvers. Subject is friend of Akhromeyev's immediate superior S.L. Sokolov, Minister of Defense. Radio intercept supplied by both NSA and Army listening station in CENSORED was supplied minutes after the argument. Details of conversation sent to CIA CENSORED department, NSA, and DIA.

Subject returned to Moscow and proceeded immediately to his office. Later attended a diplomatic function at Nigerian embassy. One of ours from CENSORED knows subject and inquired about maneuvers. Subject was evasive but stuck to old line—superiority of Soviet technology, forces, etc. Full report from agent dropped to our CENSORED department.

Subject left Saturday to his dacha outside Moscow. No sources near him. Request all available information regarding report on success and details of Soviet Rocket Force exercises.

Sources told to alert agents and officers at CENSORED to build up data on recent exercises. Other sources gathering details on exercises of Air Defense Forces, Ground Forces, and Warsaw Pact Forces. Any details related to SRFs will be passed on to CIA from DIA.

Complete file from NSA regarding cipher and radio intercepts will be forwarded after analyzed.

PLACE IN SUBJECT FILE UNDER MILITARY EXCERCISES. This file added to other information on subject: psychological, biographical, education, promotions, family, and attitudinal file.

Report No. 52 on Subject

History—1965 to 1986

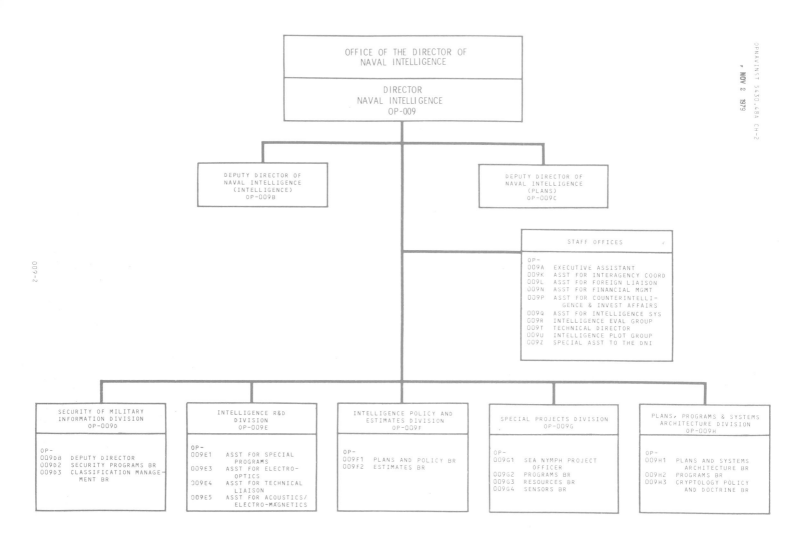

```
┌─────────────────────────────────┐
│   OFFICE OF THE DIRECTOR OF      │
│      NAVAL INTELLIGENCE          │
├─────────────────────────────────┤
│         DIRECTOR                 │
│     NAVAL INTELLIGENCE           │
│         OP-009                   │
└─────────────────────────────────┘
```

DEPUTY DIRECTOR OF NAVAL INTELLIGENCE (INTELLIGENCE) OP-009B		DEPUTY DIRECTOR OF NAVAL INTELLIGENCE (PLANS) OP-009C

STAFF OFFICES

OP-	
009A	EXECUTIVE ASSISTANT
009K	ASST FOR INTERAGENCY COORD
009L	ASST FOR FOREIGN LIAISON
009N	ASST FOR FINANCIAL MGMT
009P	ASST FOR COUNTERINTELLI- GENCE & INVEST AFFAIRS
009Q	ASST FOR INTELLIGENCE SYS
009R	INTELLIGENCE EVAL GROUP
009T	TECHNICAL DIRECTOR
009U	INTELLIGENCE PLOT GROUP
009Z	SPECIAL ASST TO THE DNI

SECURITY OF MILITARY INFORMATION DIVISION OP-009D	INTELLIGENCE R&D DIVISION OP-009E	INTELLIGENCE POLICY AND ESTIMATES DIVISION OP-009F	SPECIAL PROJECTS DIVISION OP-009G	PLANS, PROGRAMS & SYSTEMS ARCHITECTURE DIVISION OP-009H
OP- 009DB DEPUTY DIRECTOR 009D2 SECURITY PROGRAMS BR 009D3 CLASSIFICATION MANAGE-MENT BR	OP- 009E1 ASST FOR SPECIAL PROGRAMS 009E3 ASST FOR ELECTRO-OPTICS 009E4 ASST FOR TECHNICAL LIAISON 009E5 ASST FOR ACOUSTICS/ ELECTRO-MAGNETICS	OP- 009F1 PLANS AND POLICY BR 009F2 ESTIMATES BR	OP- 009G1 SEA NYMPH PROJECT OFFICER 009G2 PROGRAMS BR 009G3 RESOURCES BR 009G4 SENSORS BR	OP- 009H1 PLANS AND SYSTEMS ARCHITECTURE BR 009H2 PROGRAMS BR 009H3 CRYPTOLOGY POLICY AND DOCTRINE BR

This chart of naval intelligence operations illustrates the large extent of aerial, surface, and undersea collection. Naval intelligence also conducts counterintelligence. Unfortunately, the navy has suffered a number of espionage operations against it—the Walker case, the Morrison case, and more recently the Pollard case. In all cases, Americans worked for Soviet interests by supplying highly secret material related to naval warfare, and their motive was always monetary, not political.

Naval Intelligence

Naval intelligence is one of the oldest branches of intelligence gathering in the United States. It broke the Japanese code during World War II, which was essential to American victory in the Pacific.

The navy uses electronics ships, satellite information, computers and "field agents" to gather intelligence. Navy "seals," frogmen and frogwomen, are trained in subversive warfare, photography, sabotage, and underwater warfare.

The mission of naval intelligence covers all areas connected with naval warfare and the anticipation of warfare. It is based on: intelligence related to Soviet strategy on the high seas; submarine warfare; cryptology; counterintelligence and counterterrorism; security on American naval bases and defense con-

tractors; and gathering intelligence about Soviet naval strength and ambitions.

Of all these areas, the most important are submarine warfare and cryptology. The interception of electronic transmissions and communications between Soviet ships and naval command headquarters is paramount to any naval strategy. History has shown with operations like Ultra, Magic, and the breaking of Japanese codes that the outcome of actual battles is on the side of those who know the other's codes. Naval intelligence, therefore, relies heavily on the technological abilities of cryptology and computers which can quickly analyze and break codes.

Equally important is naval intelligence related to submarine warfare: knowing where the enemy is and where submarines are likely to attack is one of the U.S. Navy's top priorities. Among the intelligence responsibilities is the collection of information on the construction or planning of submarine bases.

Marine intelligence focuses almost exclusively on amphibious landings and on enemy strength. Recent intelligence operations in northern Norway have been a target for Soviet GRU and KGB officers. Marine guards at American embassies conduct no intelligence missions, but are always on the alert for security problems in the embassies.

Marine Corps Intelligence

Although part of the navy, the mission of the marine intelligence group is to gather intelligence related to amphibious warfare, the Marine Corps' chief field of operations.

Knowledge of beaches, harbors, and other specific targets is essential to the marines. Trained to be the first troops to land and attack, their mission might be in the realm of arctic, jungle, or desert warfare.

Gathering intelligence changes as world politics change. The focus falls on areas where the Soviets might be flexing their military muscle. If marines are training in northern Norway, near the Soviet port of Murmansk, they learn how and where Soviet troops would attack. If they face hostile Cuban troops in Guantanamo it is imperative to gather information about those enemy forces. Intelligence gathering requirements change on a day-to-day basis.

Naval intelligence satellite information from the air force supports the marine mission.

THE INTELLIGENCE MACHINE

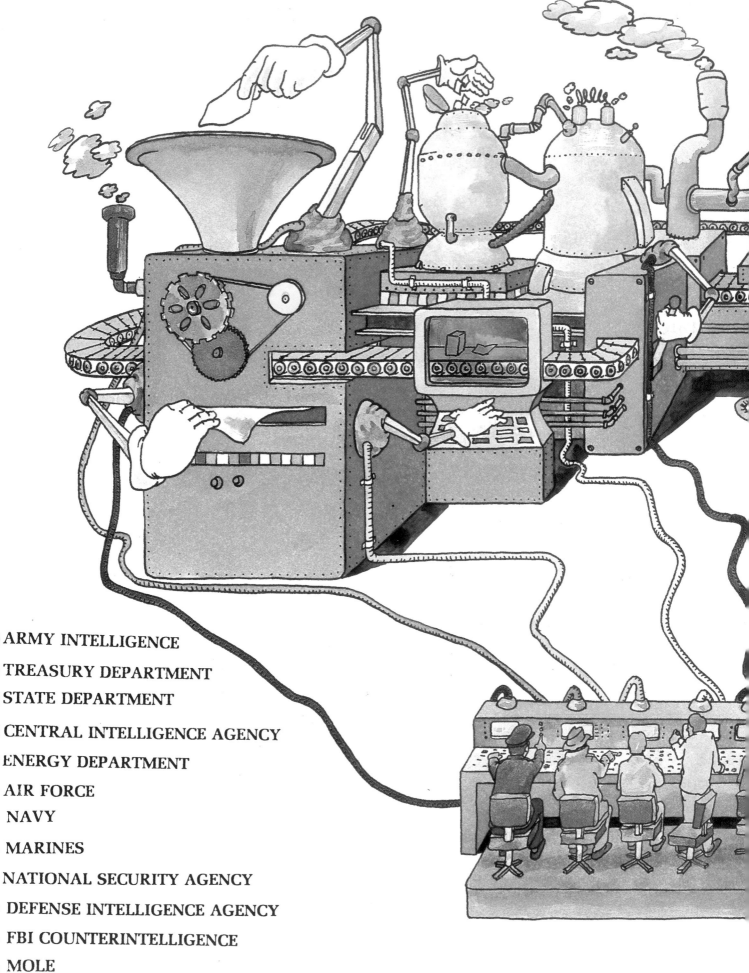

ARMY INTELLIGENCE

TREASURY DEPARTMENT

STATE DEPARTMENT

CENTRAL INTELLIGENCE AGENCY

ENERGY DEPARTMENT

AIR FORCE

NAVY

MARINES

NATIONAL SECURITY AGENCY

DEFENSE INTELLIGENCE AGENCY

FBI COUNTERINTELLIGENCE

MOLE

The air force has the largest budget for intelligence operations, mainly because of the large expense of satellites and planes, such as the SR-71 shown here. Constant 24-hour photography is taken from planes and satellites. Analysts on the ground interpret the imagery and report their findings to commanders and to CIA. The SR-71 is not only one of the sleekest and best-designed planes, it is the workhorse of the reconnaissance division of air force intelligence. The SR-71, along with the U-2, has supplied the United States with invaluable intelligence over the years. Troop movements, new Soviet missile installations, arms to Cuba, and improvements on the airfield at Grenada have all been detected by constant SR-71 overflights.

Air Force Intelligence

The air force maintains the largest intelligence program of all the services, and its Foreign Technology Division has an exhaustive assembly of intelligence and analysis of foreign aircraft and missiles.

The intelligence service operates as a separate agency providing specialized information for USAF Headquarters and air force commanders in support of planning and combat operations.

Its extensive activities are separated into different units.

The Operational Intelligence Directorate provides the service with all-source intelligence. It ensures that air force decision-makers receive accurate and comprehensive intelligence necessary to assess critical situations. It involves special research, intelligence analysis of current operations, force deployment, indications, and warning.

THE
33 CONVICTED MEMBERS
OF THE
DUQUESNE
SPY RING

The motto, "Fidelity, Bravory, Integrity," succinctly describes the motivating force behind the men and women of the FBI.

F.B.I.

The FBI agent is first and foremost a criminal investigator even if he spends a major proportion of his career gathering counterintelligence that forms a vital link in the nation's security system.

Counterintelligence is the intelligence activity devoted to protecting the U.S. against espionage, sabotage and subversion. It impedes—or better still, prevents—foreign intelligence operations conducted within the United States. While it is concerned with the hostile intentions and actions of all foreign intelligence and security systems and all individuals and groups posing a threat to the U.S., its primary reason for existence is the fight against communism.

Close cooperation between the FBI and the CIA (which operates outside the United States) is called for whenever the U.S. handles the case of a defector. When a KGB officer professes a change of heart and

defects to the American side, the FBI leads the debriefing process to establish the depth of his knowledge and gauge the genuineness of intent.

Imposing a serious threat inside the country are the number of Soviet spies engaged in clandestine activities that threaten the safety of our technological and defense secrets. While these potential dangers remain a matter of considerable concern, unchecked counterintelligence activities may also pose a threat to the country. A changing attitude by political leaders—brought about, perhaps, by the McCarthy era, which swept a tidal wave of fear through the country—has brought newly structured lines of operations to the FBI. Where it once played a dominant role in the procuring and dissemination of information concerning hostile clandestine activities, its character has now become more low-key and passive than in the

173

ESPIONAGE; INTERSTATE FLIGHT - PROBATION VIOLATION
WANTED BY FBI
EDWARD LEE HOWARD

FBI No. 720 744 CA2

4 0 1 R IIO 19
S 17 U IIO

ALIASES: Patrick Brian, Patrick M. Brian, Patrick M. Bryan, Edward L. Houston, Ed Howard, James Rogers, Roger H. Shannon, Roger K. Shannon

NCIC: DO540719191108101419

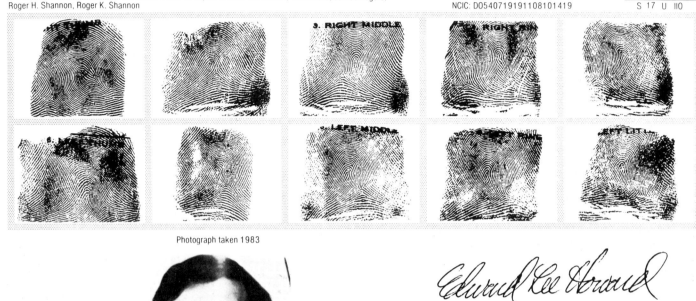

Photograph taken 1983

DESCRIPTION

DATE OF BIRTH: October 27, 1951
PLACE OF BIRTH: Alamogordo, New Mexico
HEIGHT: 5'11"
WEIGHT: 165 to 180 pounds
BUILD: medium
HAIR: brown
EYES: brown
COMPLEXION: medium
RACE: white
NATIONALITY: American
SCARS AND MARKS: 2-inch scar over right eye; scar on upper lip
OCCUPATIONS: economic analyst; former U.S. Government employee
REMARKS: Knowledgeable in the use of firearms. Reportedly speaks and understands Russian and Spanish fluently. Trained in disguise and surveillance techniques.
SOCIAL SECURITY NUMBER USED: 457-92-0226

CRIMINAL RECORD
Howard has been convicted of assault with a deadly weapon.

CAUTION
HOWARD SHOULD BE CONSIDERED ARMED AND DANGEROUS AND SHOULD BE APPROACHED WITH CAUTION INASMUCH AS HE HAS BEEN CONVICTED OF ASSAULT WITH A DEADLY WEAPON AND IS PRESENTLY ON SUPERVISED PROBATION.

William H. Webster
Director
Federal Bureau of Investigation
Washington, D.C. 20535

A Federal warrant was issued on September 23, 1985, at Albuquerque, New Mexico, charging Howard with Espionage (Title 18, U.S. Code, Section 794 (c)). A Federal warrant was also issued on September 27, 1985, at Albuquerque, New Mexico, charging Howard with Unlawful Interstate Flight to Avoid Confinement-Probation Violation (Title 18, U.S. Code, Section 1073).

IF YOU HAVE INFORMATION CONCERNING THIS PERSON, PLEASE CONTACT YOUR LOCAL FBI OFFICE. TELEPHONE NUMBERS AND ADDRESSES OF ALL FBI OFFICES LISTED ON BACK.

Identification Order 4998
October 7, 1985

This reward poster was issued within a few hours of former CIA man Edward Howard's flight from justice. The large number of aliases were probably names assigned by CIA when Howard worked for the agency. CIA has no police power even within is own agency. Howard is now believed to be living in Finland or the Soviet Union.

past. Activities have become more limited. Investigative and operational resources have decreased.

Although the full scope of the FBI has been redefined under the Reagan administration, its basic functions remain the same because only counterintelligence can contain the movements of the KGB or any other major foreign intelligence operations.

The Treasury Department conducts intelligence related to money. It has also provided the CIA with intelligence relating to cover companies using money from intelligence services, the transfer of currency to various companies, and illegal drug money laundered through U.S. banks.

Department of the Treasury

The Department of the Treasury comprises three departments, which conduct very low-level intelligence operations: the Secret Service, the U.S. Customs Service, and the Bureau of Alcohol, Tobacco, and Firearms.

Although the Secret Service's main job is to protect the President and other notables, it also has other responsibilities. These include collecting information and handling investigations into counterfeiting and forgery.

The majority of 1,500 Secret Service agents are stationed in field offices around the United States, in Puerto Rico, and in Paris.

Through the Office of Protective Intelligence, which collects, evaluates, and stores protective security data, the service keeps track of suspect individuals and groups.

The U.S. Customs Service handles investigations into such crimes as fraud, smuggling, and cargo thefts. Intelligence experts monitor the overseas production of narcotics that may eventually be smuggled into the U.S.

Special agents in the Bureau of Alcohol, Tobacco, and Firearms are involved in investigations designed to prevent and solve bombings, to discover illegal possession of explosives and firearms, and to prevent their falling into the hands of criminal elements.

Exterior view of 2,455-MW Novovoronezhskiy Atomic Power Station.

The Energy Department's intelligence service monitors and collects intelligence relating to nuclear development and also the energy needs and outputs of a nation. Energy affects a nation's economy and is essential to a nation involved in war or expanded economic development.

The Department of Energy

The Department of Energy is a source of intelligence on foreign energy matters. It collects political, economic, and technical information, some of which is produced and disseminated for other intelligence operations.

Of particular interest is the USSR, which is the richest country in the world in energy resources. Outside the Persian Gulf it has the largest oil reserves, and it is also the world's largest producer of natural gas. It has vast coal resources, and its electric output ranks second to the United States.

Although the Department of Energy provides technical and analytical research, it is chiefly a consumer of other intelligence.

Using diplomats to collect information is probably the oldest form of intelligence gathering. Today, diplomats provide the CIA, State Department, Defense Department, and other government agencies with material related to diplomacy and a nation's "diplomatic attitudes" towards the United States. One of the ablest directors of the State Department's intelligence service was former CIA Deputy Director Ray Cline. Cline (above, left) was the only CIA man ever to manage State's intelligence operation, the Bureau of Intelligence and Research (INR). Currently, State's intelligence operation is headed by Morton I. Abramowitz (above, right).

The Department of State

Within the Department of State is the Bureau of Intelligence and Research (INR). Its director is usually an ambassador serving in the bureau as a part of his career in the State Department.

It is a small, specialized intelligence unit with no agents, because while officers abroad may commonly report political intelligence, they play no part in clandestine operations.

Political and economic intelligence reports are produced within the agency for the Department of State's own needs. INR also handles the coordination of the department's relations with U.S. foreign intelligence organizations, and disseminates reports received from U.S. diplomatic and consular posts abroad.

An INR officer always plays a senior role in the production of national intelligence estimates (NIEs), which are analyzed intelligence reports from the combined efforts of all agencies. They hold interagency estimates of the political stability and military intentions of foreign countries, and are an important factor in the decision-making of the President and other policymakers.

177

Lieutenant General Eugene F. Tighe, Jr., USAF (Ret.), was Director of the Defense Intelligence Agency from 1977 to 1981. He began his military career by enlisting in the U.S. Army in 1942, serving until 1946. In 1950, he joined the U.S. Air Force as an intelligence officer. He is the recipient of many awards and decorations, including the Distinguished Service Medal and the Bronze Star. He also has the distinction of having earned his high rank while serving as an intelligence officer, a rare achievement in the U.S. military.

Q *How does the intelligence community function in relation to CIA?*

A In relation to CIA may not be the most appropriate thing, but once upon a time, the term *intelligence community* was kind of laughable because the intelligence community really was an intelligence jungle, with competition so keen and perceptions of importance, or lack thereof, and trust, or lack thereof, the order of the day. That began to change in the seventies. The post-Vietnam War era epitomized a growing cooperation among the intelligence organizations. I think a lot of that cooperation was personality driven; for example, Mr. Colby and George Bush and their successors were more driven toward a community approach than their predecessors. And of course resources had driven up the capabilities of all the Defense Department organizations in the years that were sharpened by war. And they became very potent forces in the community. So that by 1974, when I arrived in the Defense Intelligence Agency, the growing dependence of one organization on another was quite apparent and has persisted to this day and I think improved considerably. Now as far as coordination is concerned, the establishment of a staff in the middle between defense elements and the CIA was intended to bridge the gap in some way and to ensure cooperation in budgeting and a lot of other matters of importance to the whole U.S. intelligence capability.

Q *Does the personality of a particular DCI affect the efficiency of intelligence gathering, or is there an established procedure or bureaucracy that, even though one DCI may hate meetings and not have meetings, the work still gets done?*

A Well, let's say that the intelligence community is a great survivor and has a tremendous amount of experience. And it has outlived all the DCIs. But I have nothing but praise for all the DCIs I've known, and I've known them all since Dulles, and I knew him well. But the personality does drive the activities of the intelligence community in one or the other direction. And if it sets up competing bodies of influence in that community it wastes an awful lot of their business on fighting one another or fighting him or resisting him, and it does the nation a lot of harm. It's very difficult to change the practices of a community that is as entrenched and as large as the U.S. intelligence community. Especially because most of the country thinks intelligence organizations don't do anything except go out and assassinate people and carry on dirty tricks around the world, when in fact 99 percent of the activities of the intelligence community are producing foreign intelligence, collecting and analyzing for the basis of decision-making in the White House and the State Department.

Q *Just a small percentage of it, then, is the covert—*

A Well, none of it is involved in assassinations—that's illegal. But covert activity is a tiny, tiny, little bit of the activity.

Q *Is there one DCI that you think has done more for the service, has been the best there's ever been?*

A No, I wouldn't say that. I think as far as how much they've done for the community, it's a matter of tenure, how long have they been on the job. Each one of them had a different personality, and they had different challenges. Mr. Colby had to fess up to activities of the Central Intelligence Agency over which he had no control. And he had to be the bad guy among a lot of people who think he told too much.

Q *Do the variety of collection procedures and all the agencies CIA coordinates with overload CIA? Can CIA do the work it's supposed to do efficiently because of the vast amount of information it's dealing with?*

A We have an IC staff, an intelligence community staff, that does a lot of that activity of setting up requirements and levying responsibilities on the organizations. And the coordination at the National Foreign Intelligence Board level by the agency chiefs of their plan for the next year or the next five years isn't all that time consuming. The principals are briefed by committee structures for each of the segments of this business—signals intelligence, for example, photographic intelligence, and so forth—so it's a fairly smooth process that doesn't require a tremendous amount of time on the part of the principals, if they are knowledgeable intelligence officers.

Q *When the CIA got a lot of criticism in the 1970s, did that in any way affect what the CIA did then compared to what it does now?*

A I don't think so. I would suggest that there was a time when through lack of coordination and the usual jealousies in that jungle I was talking about, CIA and the other agencies spent more time fighting one another and trying to take things away from one another or keep things from one another. Of course it's quite the opposite today. They try to give each other functions or get some support from each other for what they're doing. So I would suggest the Defense Intelligence Agency, for example, has a charter to take over all military intelligence in peacetime. And they have a very nice checks and balances system created within the intelligence structure of the country. The Defense Intelligence Agency does political and economic analysis. They're not the principal economic and political analysts. State Department is the principal economic and political analyst. But each has the right to do a little bit of analysis on the other's rice bowl. For example, the Central Intelligence Agency is very heavily engaged in doing military analysis and defense analysis, sufficiently so, so that there's a nice check and balance, and when the whole community gets together and writes a national estimate, there is that kind of coordination that allows for balance. And it keeps one organization from absolutely having the say-so over what's going on. There's been a lot of criticism, for example from time to time in the press, intimating that the national estimates are made to support budgeting. For example, the strategic estimate on the Soviet Union, the military estimate, is a year-round process. It's going on day after day, it's such a huge endeavor that covers offensive weapons as well as defensive. There's no cycle whatsoever that coincides with any budgetary cycle, I can assure you.

Q *You were recently elected president of the Association of Former Intelligence Officers. Can you tell me a little about this organization?*

A David Phillips started AFIO, as you know, and our purpose is to help the active intelligence community where they can't speak for themselves; they've got to stay silent on a lot of things. And secondly, we try to educate our youth being educated in the colleges and universities of the country through various and sundry means of the importance of a good foreign intelligence capability for the United States. And that 3,500-member organization now—it's grown from very small beginnings—represents the alumni of the CIA, the FBI, the Defense Intelligence Agency, the military intelligence agencies, and so forth. And it's very effective, operating all over the world in many chapters. And the point that I want to make in all this is that there is a strong support in this country for a good intelligence establishment. And that strong support also demands that it be an ethical and a very Constitutional and legal apparatus, and that's why we're going to stay strong, because we are pushed by the people of the country who tell their congressmen whether to fund the establishment or not. And the alumni association is terribly important, I think, to the progress and support of the establishment.

179

Watch Dogs

"COMRADES, THE PROBLEM ISN'T GETTING THE INFORMATION ITS FIGURING OUT WHICH IS CORRECT."

CIA

The White House has the ultimate responsibility for oversight of CIA

Watch Dogs

Designed in the mid-1950's by the New York firm of Harrison and Abramovitz the CIA headquarters building was envisioned by the then Director Allen W. Dulles as having the atmosphere of a college campus.

CIA Watch Dogs

Unlike most foreign intelligence agencies, the Central Intelligence Agency is subject to a number of outside forces that monitor and call the agency to task for performing outside its charter.

The United States is a democracy based on a system of checks and balances. The executive, legislative, and judicial branches serve to work together, compromise, and check each other. In this delicate and often complicated democratic mixture, the Central Intelligence Agency is also involved. The agency operates under the executive branch and is responsible to the President and any informal or presidential advisors the Chief Executive decides should interface with the CIA.

In addition to the President, some Vice-Presidents take an active and daily interest in intelligence matters.

In addition to the President and the Vice-President there are, (1) the National Security Council, (2) the President's Foreign Intelligence Advisory Board, (3) the Intelligence Oversight Board, (4) the Senate Select Committee on Intelligence, (5) the House Permanent Committee on Intelligence, (6) the House and Senate Appropriations Committee, and (7) the Office of Management and Budget. These formal congressional operations can be further tested by the federal court system. Thus, the judiciary also plays a role.

In the political system there are also non-governmental "watchdogs" as well. These are first and foremost the American people, the American press and its legion of newspapers, radio, and television

183

President Reagan, breaking ground for CIA headquarters addition in May, 1984. Both the President and the Vice-President meet frequently with the Director of Central Intelligence to discuss a wide variety of intelligence matters.

George Bush as a former Director of the CIA has a unique insight into intelligence matters. As Vice-President his role is both "watchdog" and government leader on intelligence.

broadcasts, publishing houses, and thousands of reporters and editors. In addition, the Soviet Intelligence Service—the KGB—is always interested in intelligence matters.

The following gives an example how each of these functions.

The President and Vice-President

The President meets with the Director of Central Intelligence frequently. What is discussed? The Director of Central Intelligence keeps the President informed of all major intelligence activities and any discoveries as a result of CIA or other intelligence community activities. In addition, the Director

The Capitol building symbolizes a number of congressional watchdog groups.

Presidents Eisenhower, Kennedy and Johnson used the intelligence services as part of their foreign policy. Each had major successes but also major intelligence snafu's — Eisenhower — the U-2 incident, Kennedy — the Bay of Pigs, and Johnson — the Gulf of Tonkin incident. All of them strongly believed in extensive use of the clandestine arm of the CIA. After Johnson most Presidents have become reluctant to overly use covert activities.

informs the President of any new photographic intelligence affecting the security of the United States. Some secret intelligence developments eventually become known to the public. The Cuban missile crisis during President Kennedy's term or the discoveries of accelerated Soviet and Cuban military moves in Grenada during President Reagan's term are examples. In addition, the President can ask the Director to initiate specific intelligence activities. Recent Presidents have restricted such activities, although President Reagan has been an exception. During the administrations of Presidents Eisenhower, Kennedy, and Johnson these activities were often part and parcel of American foreign policy. This is not to say clandestine activities today are not performed under tight control.

Robert Murphy and Stephen Ailes former secretary of the Army; were the first members of an intelligence oversight board.

Dr. Albert Wheelon serves as a member of President Reagan's Foreign Intelligence Advisory Board. Dr. Wheelon's watchdog role is to support, criticize and recommend changes to strengthen the intelligence community.

President's Foreign Intelligence Advisory Board (PFIAB)

The PFIAB is maintained within the Executive Office of the President. Its several members serve at the pleasure of the President and are appointed from among trustworthy and distinguished American citizens outside of government, who are qualified on the basis of achievement, experience, and independence. They serve without compensation. The board continually reviews the performance of *all* government agencies engaged in the collection, evaluation, or production of intelligence or in the execution of intelligence policy. It also assesses the adequacy of management, personnel, and organization in intel-

POINT SALINES AIRFIELD, GRENADA

10,000 FOOT RUNWAY

POL STORAGE AREA

SUPPORT AREA

BARRACKS AREA

The Point Salines airfield was defended by members of the Cuban DGI—the Cuban Intelligence Service.

Photographic changes indicated a threat to national security when it was noted and reported that Soviet and Cubans were increasing military capability in Grenada. Human agents also reported Grenada was being established as a military base for the Cubans and their allies. Based on these intelligence reports President Reagan and our allies took action.

ligence agencies; and advises the President concerning the objectives, conduct, and coordination of the activities of these agencies. The PFIAB is specifically charged to make appropriate recommendations for actions to improve and enhance the performance of the intelligence efforts of the United States; this advice may be passed directly to the Director of Central Intelligence, the Central Intelligence Agency, or other heads of agencies engaged in intelligence activities.

Intelligence Oversight Board (IOB)

The President's Intelligence Oversight Board functions within the White House. The IOB consists

The electronic spying operation at Lourdes in Cuba employs 2100 Soviet and Cuban technicians. The CIA is a target for such eavesdropping.

William Casey perhaps the last DCI who was one of "Wild Bill" Donovan's OSS men, is the first DCI who has to answer to and be responsible to so many watchdog groups. The amount of administrative time spent testifying and briefing government and media leaders has increased dramatically since the 1970's.

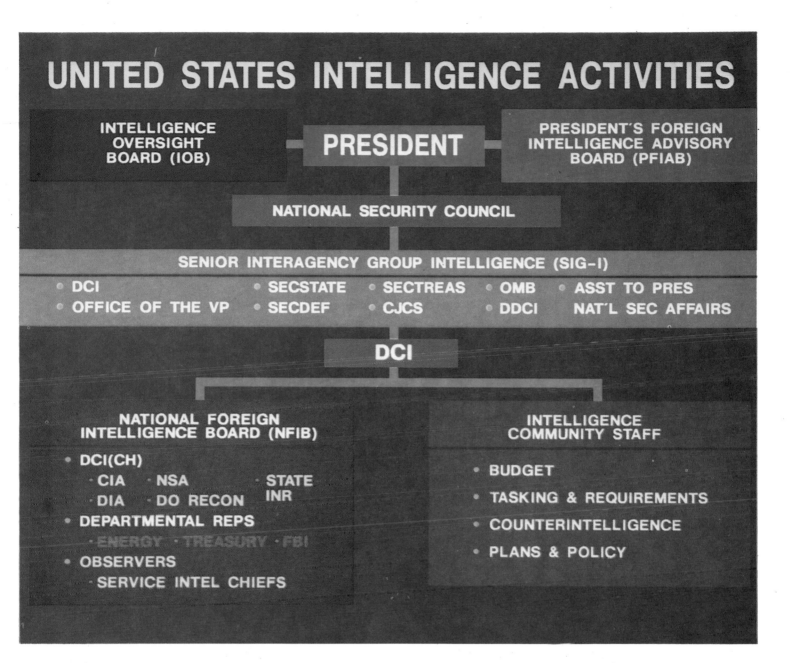

UNITED STATES INTELLIGENCE ACTIVITIES

INTELLIGENCE OVERSIGHT BOARD (IOB)

PRESIDENT

PRESIDENT'S FOREIGN INTELLIGENCE ADVISORY BOARD (PFIAB)

NATIONAL SECURITY COUNCIL

SENIOR INTERAGENCY GROUP INTELLIGENCE (SIG-I)
- DCI
- OFFICE OF THE VP
- SECSTATE
- SECDEF
- SECTREAS
- CJCS
- OMB
- DDCI
- ASST TO PRES
- NAT'L SEC AFFAIRS

DCI

NATIONAL FOREIGN INTELLIGENCE BOARD (NFIB)
- DCI(CH)
  - CIA · NSA · STATE INR
  - DIA · DO RECON
- DEPARTMENTAL REPS
  - ENERGY · TREASURY · FBI
- OBSERVERS
  - SERVICE INTEL CHIEFS

INTELLIGENCE COMMUNITY STAFF
- BUDGET
- TASKING & REQUIREMENTS
- COUNTERINTELLIGENCE
- PLANS & POLICY

This chart illustrates the often complex and bureaucratic structure of United States intelligence. Within this network there are hundreds of specialized departments employing several hundred thousand employees.

of three members from outside the government who are appointed by the President. One of these, who serves as chairman, is also a member of the President's Foreign Intelligence Advisory Board. The IOB is responsible for discovering and reporting to the President any intelligence activities that raise questions of impropriety or illegality in terms of the Constitution, the laws of the U.S., or Presidential Executive Order. The board is also charged with reviewing the internal guidelines and direction of the intelligence community.

National Security Council (NSC)

The NSC was established by the National Security Act of 1947 to advise the President with respect to the

President Kennedy is shown here with members of the National Security Council during the Cuban Missile Crisis. Intelligence reports were the reason for the meeting.

President Truman was the first President to end an intelligence agency — OSS in 1945 and to start one — the CIA. President Truman is shown signing the National Security Act of 1947 which established the Central Intelligence Agency.

integration of domestic, foreign, and military policies relating to the national security. The NSC is the highest executive branch entity—other than the President himself—providing review of, guidance for, and direction to the conduct of all national foreign intelligence and counterintelligence activities. The statutory members of the NSC are the President, the Vice-President, the Secretary of State, the Secretary of Defense, and others the President may designate. The Director of Central Intelligence and the Chairman of the Joint Chiefs of Staff participate as advisors. The same 1947 Act also established the CIA as an independent agency subordinate to the NSC.

Senior Interagency Group (SIG)

This committee of the NSC is composed variously of the Director of Central Intelligence, the Assistant to

OUR GREAT SYSTEM WAS FOUNDED ON TRUST AND LOYALTY COMRADE, WE DO NOT NEED WATCHDOGS LIKE THOSE CAPITALISTS.

Shortly after the Bay of Pigs debacle President Kennedy relieved director Allen Dulles and brought in Republican John McCone as DCI and to reorganize the CIA "operations" department.

the President for National Security Affairs, the Deputy Secretary of State, the Deputy Secretary of Defense, the Chairman of the Joint Chiefs of Staff, the Deputy Attorney General, the Director of the Federal Bureau of Investigation, and the Director of the National Security Agency. The SIG chairman varies according to the meeting agenda, for example, the Director of Central Intelligence is chairman when the body addresses intelligence matters. The SIG (Intelligence) is charged to advise and assist the NSC in discharging its authority and responsibility for intelligence policy and intelligence matters. It ensures that important intelligence policy issues requiring interagency attention receive full, prompt, and systematic coordination. It also monitors the execution of previously approved policies and decisions.

Leo Cherne serves as vice-chairman on the President's Foreign Intelligence Advisory Board. He is also executive director of the Research Institute of America and executive chairman of Freedom House, an organization to advance the struggle for freedom.

Q *What does PFIAB do?*
A We were created by executive order of the President. It's a group designed to stand up to the CIA and to the President, if necessary. We report directly to the President or the National Security Advisor. We are an independent group with no outside forces pressuring us. We are a nonpartisan advisory board on intelligence.

Q *Are you a secret group?*
A Not secret, but the matters we discuss are secret. They have to be secret, they are involved with intelligence. I also want to be very careful what I tell you as PFIAB has agreed not to divulge matters relating to what we do. These matters are both confidential in the act of working for the country at the President's request and because of intelligence.

Q *Are your meetings held in tight security?*
A Absolutely—very excellent security, and leakproof. We must have top security.

Q *Are you a KGB target?*
A Definitely. The KGB would love to know what we do. They would give their right arm to find out about us.

Q *Why doesn't the public know about the PFIAB?*
A We get very little attention. The press goes after what are really small aspects of intelligence—espionage, defectors, et cetera.

Q *How did you get involved?*
A I met Richard Nixon in 1951, and although I wasn't of his political party and not a supporter, he made some contacts for me. I was also with International Rescue Committee and met Bill Donovan. It was at the time of the Hungarian Uprising in 1956.

Q *How does PFIAB work?*
A I will try to answer your question without revealing too much. The nature of our work falls into several categories: (1) The President asks us to do things; (2) We work with elements within the intelligence community; (3) We study and make recommendations for change or improvement. As far as oversight, we do not, and I repeat *do not*, get involved with behavior of the intelligence agencies. Our part of oversight is not concerned with means or behavior. We are concerned with the quality of the reporting, the analysis, of the entire state of intelligence. Is our technical collection the best? Is our analysis the best?

Q *How are you selected?*
A We are selected by the President. Each president selects a different board and the goals are often the direction that President takes. Each board differs. Its importance differs. Some Presidents are actively involved. Some, as President Carter, don't want a PFIAB. You see, we are critics. No one in government wants another body looking over his shoulder critiquing him.

But over the years, PFIAB has made crucial decisions and recommendations which have improved our CIA and intelligence community.

Q *How?*
A Well, I have reservations about talking with you. Our work is secret. Very secret. But some things come out. I'll give you one example. After our recommendations, the CIA has established the A team, B team plan. This is having two separate groups go after or, say, analyze intelligence. It's worked very well. It's all designed in our democratic process to make information accurate so a President can make decisions.

Q *What does the future hold for the CIA?*
A Intelligence and the size of the world's intelligence communities will increase. We are an interdependent world. Conflict is increasing and problems are growing and growing for the U.S. We are being challenged from several areas: (1) More nations—third world nations—are developing their technology and economies; (2) Debt from many nations is enormous; (3) The USSR is making steady economic progress—slow but steady.

Q *Does this pose a threat, as they use their resources to expand?*
A Yes, and they will feel stronger at home to get involved in more adventures. This is why we need better analysis and better intelligence.

Q *What area has been most neglected?*
A For many years economic intelligence. We got into this late. We have improved our knowledge and decision-making, but we need to keep improving.

Interagency Groups (IGs)

The new J. Edgar Hoover FBI building.

To assist the SIG (Intelligence), Interagency Groups have been established to consider individual policy issues. Each IG consists of representatives of the SIG members and, upon invitation of the IG chairman, others with specific responsibilities for matters being considered. A representative of the Director of Central Intelligence chairs meetings dealing with national foreign intelligence. A representative of the Federal Bureau of Investigation chairs meetings dealing with domestic counterintelligence, except for international terrorism, which is divided between a State Department representative for terrorism abroad and an Attorney General representative for terrorism in the U.S. An indeterminate number of IGs may be designated by the SIG to address such policy issues. The IGs, in turn, may establish working groups as needed to provide support to the approved mechanisms of the NSC for such matters.

The Senate

The Senate Select Committee on Intelligence was formed during the mid-1970s. The purpose was to investigate alleged abuses in the intelligence community. The committee was formed due to the report of abuses against private citizens mentioned in the Rockefeller report commissioned by President Ford. Many Americans felt this was a sensational

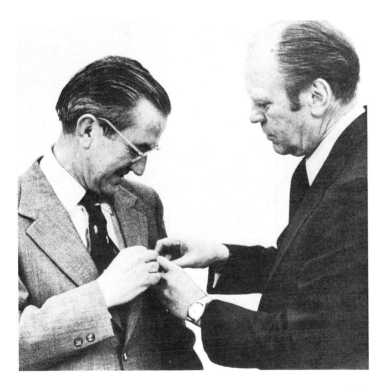

Time magazine cover of September 1974 roasted Director William Colby. The interrogations of the DCI began.

This photo shows Senator John McClellan questioning former Director Helms and Director Colby. Both DCI's acquitted themselves well against several hostile congressmen. Intelligence agencies abroad were shocked at this uniquely American investigation into our "spy" agencies. At the time critics accused Helms of not saying enough and Colby of saying too much. In retrospect both proved to be honest and capable and the investigations helped create the basis for "watchdog" groups. Many of the ideas were recommended and adopted by both Helms and Colby.

witch-hunt which spent over $3 million and had over 150 staff members investigating the intelligence community. After the initial investigations — which undoubtedly hurt the image of the intelligence community and hindered much of its daily operations — the Senate selected Senator Daniel K. Inouye to be the committee's first chairman. Thanks to his efforts, and later to those of Senator Barry Goldwater, the respect between Congress and the intelligence community seems to be restored.

How did the Committee First Operate?

When Senator Goldwater first joined what was called the Church Committee in 1975 the committee

had disrupted the activities of the Central Intelligence Agency. The committee and the media brought out questionable activities—all ordered by Presidents of the United States. During this period, the Central Intelligence Agency was criticized, attacked, and questioned. It damaged the agency in two major respects: First, operations were exposed which hampered the government's ability to collect needed intelligence. Second, this undermining gave the impression to the American people that the CIA was spying on its citizenry, was doing "bad," un-American things overseas, and had in fact often failed in its missions. This led the American public to look unfavorably on the agency. It also indirectly with help of the press made the opposition—KGB—look 10 feet

CIA WATCHDOGS

No other intelligence agency in the world is subjected to as much scrutiny as the CIA. In many ways this hinders operations that should be kept secret and raises questions about how well security can be maintained.

The following chart gives an idea of the number of people involved in scrutinizing intelligence operations of the CIA and, by comparison, two of its major counterparts.

INTELLIGENCE AGENCY	WATCHDOG	STAFF INVOLVED
Central Intelligence Agency	Executive Office of the President	President, Vice-President, secretaries, assistants. Total: 10
	President's Foreign Intelligence Advisory Board	Total: 14
	Intelligence Oversight Board	Total: 3
	Senate Select Committee	Total: 20
	(Original Church Committee)	(Total: 150)
	House Select Committee	Total: 16
	Office of Management and Budget	Classified
	Press	More than 200 American reporters who cover intelligence
	Judiciary	One federal judge plus court staff. Total: usually 5
	KGB	Unknown
		TOTAL KNOWN WATCHDOGS: 268
British Secret Service	Minister of Defense	Total: 1
Soviet KGB	It answers to no watchdog	—

The "watchdog chart" illustrates the President's role and those commitees responsible for monitoring intelligence activities. KGB goals are to get close to the watchdog groups, penetrate if possible and spy on secretaries, members of Congress and anyone gathering information relating to the intelligence community. The "watchdog" groups have become a new and top priority target for the Soviets.

Not much is known about KGB operations related to the CIA Watchdogs but more and more information has been revealed about KGB operations to discredit the CIA. The KGB uses false agents, disinformation campaigns and uses wiretapping, and other technological apparatus to monitor and disrupt CIA activities. Their top priority is to get a Soviet mole into the ranks or leadership of the CIA. In addition to CIA penetration attempts they are constantly attempting penetration of American universities, think-tanks, government agencies and the FBI and military intelligence. Whether stealing technolgical secrets or placing "agents of influence", the KGB is operating full strength against the United States.

The new Soviet Embassy in Washington, D.C., sits atop the highest piece of land with direct access to the White House, the Pentagon, and Congress. It will serve as a better watchdog for technical and photographic collection. The National Security Agency, however, is countering Soviet collection efforts with jamming and blocking.

Senator Frank Church and Senator John Tower. Church holds up a special dart pistol created for CIA agents.

Congressman Otis Pike probably did more damage during the hearings than anyone.

The CIA suffered during the Church committee "witch-hunt". Most alleged abuses proved groundless. With media coverage and KGB disinformation campaigns the American public frowned on covert action and assassination attempts. Many intelligence officers feel although this period initially hurt secret operations, the maturing of the American people toward intelligence began. Today, with constant revelations of Soviet espionage in America and Soviet disinformation campaigns more of the American people realize the importance of the total intelligence community.

tall. It didn't matter if the KGB was doing everything to hurt the American people—the fact is they looked like winners.

In a survey taken in 1985 among high school juniors and seniors, this attitude seems to linger.

As Senator Goldwater became more involved, tremendous strides were made by the committee to both monitor the agency and keep the channels for good intelligence gathering open. Goldwater and the committee streamlined the operation, did more to protect covert agents abroad, passed legislation prohibiting the publication of agents names, and did as much as possible to let the CIA perform its mission— the collection of foreign intelligence.

The House of Representatives

The House of representatives does the same type of congressional monitoring as the Senate. Its committee members are selected by seniority. The Director of

Many of the abuses created by intelligence activities were initiated by Presidents of the United States. Most Presidents thought of the CIA as supermen who could accomplish anything that diplomacy could not. President Kennedy in his brief 3 years as President initiated more CIA operations for covert action than any Chief Executive.

Central Intelligence is responsible for keeping the committee informed on all aspects of the intelligence community's activities and for supplying specific information requested by the committee.

Safeguards

In the past the tendency was to think of the Central Intelligence Agency as operating entirely on its own without supervision of its activities. Perhaps this tendency grew from the fact that much of the agency's work must be kept secret, thus making total public oversight an impossibility.

Though total public oversight is indeed an impossibility, several safeguards exist which control Central Intelligence Agency actions. They provide each citizen, or members of the intelligence community, an avenue through which concerns, complaints, or questions can be brought to light and examined.

HIS SPY GLASS

This historical print demonstrates that even during World War I foreign powers, in this case Germany, were keeping an eye on attitudes in the United States.

The first of these safeguards is in the White House. The President and Vice-President take an active and daily interest in intelligence efforts. The Director of Central Intelligence meets with them regularly to keep them informed.

The second is the Intelligence Oversight Board, whose three members are appointed by the President from the public sector and report directly to him. Created in 1976, the board will hear anyone, from within or outside of the federal government and will promise that person anonymity. It will look at each issue raised and determine whether or not it warrants action. It then reports its findings to the President.

The third safeguard is congressional. The Senate Select Committee on Intelligence and the House

Admiral Stansfield Turner is a 1946 graduate of the United States Naval Academy, and was also a Rhodes scholar, receiving a master's degree in philosophy, politics and economics from Oxford University in 1950. He rose to become commander of NATO's Southern Flank. In 1977, President Jimmy Carter appointed him Director of Central Intelligence, a post he held until 1981.

Q *Admiral Turner, always the main question for DCIs—should we use covert action, and how?*

A It is a very necessary tool that we must use in an opportune way. However, opportunities are usually extremely limited. It must be used judiciously and the question is, can it stay covert in a democracy?

Q *What about oversight and covert action?*

A The oversight process is necessary. Poor oversight has resulted in a number of foreign failures—the French secret service and Greenpeace, the West German spy case, and the recent Israeli spy case in this country. It's controversial in the intelligence community because of leaks, but covert action and oversight can go together and serve as a part of American foreign policy.

Q *You were the first DCI in a very long time to come to direct the intelligence community without any background in intelligence. What was it like?*

A When I came to CIA, the agency was still under the spectre of the abuses—mail openings, domestic spying, and the Nosenko defector case. I tried to move the CIA ahead and do its job—the collection of intelligence. I began the reorganization and streamlining of intelligence departments. This had been initiated under former DCI James Schlesinger. At one time there were four separate personnel departments—too much departmental independence and other things that needed changes.

Q *Was the Iranian hostage crisis all-consuming?*

A Yes. It was taking about 70 percent of my time. But in my entire career, both in the Navy and at CIA, there is nothing I am more proud of than our providing intelligence during that time. Even though the military portion failed, our intelligence was the greatest. CIA did a superb job.

Q *Is it true we had hundreds of operatives in Iran posing as businessmen, Irishmen, et cetera?*

A I cannot comment on that.

Q *Were most of the hostages CIA?*

A I won't comment on that. I will say this: During my term as DCI, we initiated more covert operations and general operations than the previous administration.

Q *Admiral, you are known as the person who expanded the scientific and technological collection of CIA and reduced the clandestine service.*

A This is ridiculous. Science and technology always have been moving ahead; American progress. And we are ahead of the Soviets.

Q *Light years ahead?*

A No, not light years, but way ahead. The technical collection area is superb and getting better, but I didn't focus all my time and effort there. I am criticized for chopping the espionage section. I eliminated 805 spaces not by firings, but by not rehiring, and the fact is, many CIA espionage people were near retirement. It was overstaffed and this was blown out of proportion.

Q *What were your three major contributions?*

A First, bringing community to the intelligence community. The DCI is not only head of CIA but also the other intelligence agencies. Through better coordination, relations between the various departments improved. Second, bringing management to the CIA. Third, adapting the intelligence community to oversight. Making oversight and intelligence work complement each other. Very important in our democracy, with our tradition of freedoms and values. Extremely difficult when you're dealing with a secret organization.

Q *Do you think the majority of Congress understands what the CIA does?*

A No.

Q *Is it likely that there will be more KGB defectors?*

A Yes. As their (Soviet) society becomes more open and information about our way of life spreads, there will be even more. Moreover, our intelligence system with more openness, better technology, and oversight is superior to the KGB.

Q *It sounds like you are playing down the human element of spying.*

A Not at all. It's very important and will continue to be. It's just that certain aspects of technology supplement it and free the human aspect to do other things.

Q *What about the future of the CIA?*

A My agenda for action is: (1) Convince the intelligence community that good oversight is essential to effective intelligence. (2) Better analysis—the CIA should have analysts who have lived in the country, speak the language, etc. (3) Separate the roles of the DCI from that of head of the intelligence community; they conflict. (4) Merge the espionage and analytic branches of the CIA. (5) Strengthen the DCI's authority over the National Security Agency. (6) Stop leaks of information. (7) Depoliticize the role of the DCI. (8) Reduce the emphasis on covert action. (9) Be more open; it's the greatest strength our democracy has over the Soviets.

"OH, THEY WERE JUST WAITING FOR THE LATEST DECLASSIFIED F.O.I.A. REPORTS SIR."

Today many publishers are entering the growing spy and intelligence field. The books by Marchetti and Marks, Philip Agee, and Frank Snepp set the intelligence community scurrying to cover itself. Today the CIA uses the courts to test American law related to intelligence information.

Permanent Select Committee on Intelligence have primary congressional responsibility for overseeing all intelligence activities. The House and Senate Appropriations Committees review intelligence activities to assure that they are cost effective. These four committees exercise a true oversight function by scrutinizing the Central Intelligence Agency's work on a continuing basis and providing advice and guidance when appropriate. The agency reports to them in considerable detail and is completely responsive to their requests for information regarding intelligence activities.

The Central Intelligence Agency is an intelligence organization working primarily abroad on behalf of the U.S. government. It collects, analyzes, and dis-seminates foreign intelligence. It has no law enforcement powers, and its budget is carefully scrutinized by the Office of Management and Budget, even if it is not made public. While its failures are often trumpeted, its successes seldom receive fanfare because they usually must remain secret. The Central Intelligence Agency has changed mightily since its inception. Today it walks a new and fine line between openness in government Americans have come to expect and the secrecy that intelligence, by its very nature, demands.

Although the chart indicates that many people from the government are involved in monitoring intelligence activities, most security leaks have been caused by the media and private citizens, acting on their own.

LETTER FROM THE EDITOR-IN-CHIEF:

Disinformation: Twisted facts distort reality

President Reagan told The Washington Post last week that "we've been subjected, in this country, to a very sophisticated lobbying campaign by a totalitarian government — the Sandinistas. There has been a disinformation program that is virtually worldwide, and we know that the Soviets and Cubans have such a disinformation network that is beyond anything we can match."

The Post in particular, and the liberal media in general, dismisses the very notion of Soviet and Soviet-bloc disinformation as a manifestation of paranoia about communism. In a column headlined "Sandinista Disinformation?" — the question mark was designed to discredit the president's irrefutable statement of fact — The Post's deputy editorial page director, Stephen S. Rosenfeld, wrote, in effect, "Yes, but so what?"

So a lot, Mr. Rosenfeld.

Vietnamese officials (e.g., General Giap himself) and defectors have confirmed that disinformation operations in crucial role in laying the groundwork for yet another U.S. strategic defeat.

There are many groups in the United States whose media connections are an open secret. Their mission is to shade, embroider, and distort the truth for their own disinformation agenda, while excoriating anyone else who is less than truthful. These groups have helped nurture an entire new generation of journalists who have made it their duty to transform America's sworn enemies into misunderstood innocents, while at the same time portraying our own leaders as the foes of democracy and freedom.

Apologists for communism in Cuba, Vietnam, Angola, Mozambique, Ethiopia, Nicaragua, Afghanistan and elsewhere have argued that they were driven down the Marxist path of hostility because of abuse by the U.S. government. That this is sheer, unadulterated disinformation is confirmed by communist dissidents and defectors, yet it is still eagerly regurgitated by the liberal establishment on both sides of the

An example of recent misinformation sponsored by the Soviets.

In a sense there are watchdogs who monitor the KGB — as many KGB operators spy on each other. In political reality only the Praesidium can monitor or serve as a watchdog. It is unlikely that Premier Gorbachev will be able to curtail KGB abuses and power and many CIA analysts believe he will expand KGB operations — especially in the U.S.

KGB

Senator Barry Goldwater in 1983 stated, "I wish we could try to do to the Soviet KGB what we tried to do to ourselves." Although it is hard to document the activities of the KGB, certain facts are known about its operations. The successful book *KGB: The Secret Work of Soviet Secret Agents*, by John Barron, gives the first true glimpse of some of its activities. Also, the publication by the Association of Former Intelligence Officers, *The KGB: Instrument of Soviet Power* by Thomas Polgar, gives much insight into its activities. Unfortunately, there has not been published one good book or study about the KGB and its efforts to penetrate the CIA watchdogs and the CIA.

What is known is that they prowl the halls of Congress and other government departments. Unfortunately, in an open democratic society little can be done. Second, they encourage misinformation which can cause confusion, anxiety, and consternation among government agencies. Third, they try to place themselves in positions close to those involved in intelligence—committee members, secretaries, aides, newspaper reporters, and so forth. Fourth, they financially back and otherwise support American citizens and former agents who seek to sensationalize and expose CIA activities. Nothing promotes the political objectives of the Soviet Union more than to make the Central Intelligence Agency look bad and to encourage investigations in order to distract the agency from its goals.

"CIA Watchdogs" the only missing component is the Soviet GRU — the
military intelligence agency. The GRU has been the new and aggressive
organization directed against CIA. The East Bloc countries as well as the
Cuban DGI could also be included.

Philip Agee has become a leading critic of the CIA.

Private citizens can also monitor the CIA although resources to do such are costly and the motives of individual Americans investigating the CIA become suspect.

Private Citizens

Unfortunately, most CIA exposures have come from private citizens—probably backed by the KGB or members of Communist intelligence agencies.

The names of more than 1,000 alleged CIA officers were also disclosed in two books by former CIA officer Philip Agee. Louis Wolf, the co-editor of *The Covert Action Information Bulletin* to which Agee contributes, claims it disclosed the names of more than 2,000 CIA officers over a six-year period.

The danger of such exposure was underscored by incidents of violence in Greece, Jamaica, and Nicaragua. Richard Welch, CIA Station Chief in

Andropov, who directed the KGB for more than 15 years, expanded KGB intelligence gathering on CIA watchdog groups.

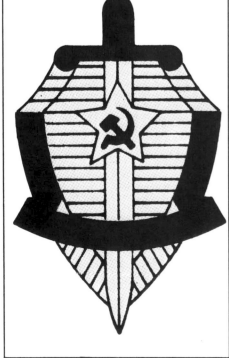

Athens, was shot and killed in front of his home in December 1975, less than a month after he was identified in *Athens Daily News*. His name was publicly circulated earlier by a magazine then published by Agee.

On July 4, 1980, in Kingston, Jamaica, shots were fired into the home of an American embassy official, Richard Kinsman, only 48 hours after editor Wolf named Kinsman and 14 other American diplomats in a Jamaica press conference as alleged agents of the CIA. On July 7, 1980, three days after Kinsman's home was machine-gunned and bombed, another embassy employee listed by Wolf apparently was targeted but escaped without harm. In addition to the disclosure of

During 1981 Agee visited Nicaragua (he is a frequent visitor) and tried to identify CIA staff. At the same time the Sandinistas organized a demonstration against American foreign policy. Reorganizing and pulling out agents cost millions of dollars and disrupted operations. Among left-wing publishers he is the expert on the CIA in Latin America.

Former CIA officer Philip Agee is shown at the head of a demonstration in London in 1977. The British government ordered him deported. Agee wrote a book exposing CIA operations.

names, Wolf also made public the addresses, telephone numbers, automobile license plate numbers, and even the colors of automobiles driven by the Americans he cited.

On November 6, 1981, several weeks after Philip Agee visited Nicaragua and charged at a press conference that at least 10 CIA agents were "hiding" in the U.S. embassy's Political Section, four American officials were listed as CIA agents in a progovernment newspaper in Managua. Thereafter, all four were harassed by armed men. Between November 6 and December 13, 1981, three women employees at the embassy were assaulted, bound, and gagged by armed men who overpowered the guards and broke into their homes in Managua.

SCIENCE AND TECHNOLOGY

So much has been heard, rumored, and published about the advanced state of science as it has been applied to our more esoteric intelligence gathering mechanisms, such as spy satellites, U-2s, special night-flying birds, and Glomarlike activities, that many tend to forget that there do exist other technologies dedicated to supporting the human intelligence (HUMINT) collector. CIA's successes in employing the tools of clandestinity, a practice often associated with trying and hazardous circumstances, waxes and wanes according to the imagination, courage, and tolerance for pain and disappointment of the systems developers, the case officers using the tools, and senior Washington managers. Nonetheless, American scientific whiz kids are as active as ever.

The U.S. intelligence technical effort that took root in the late 1940s was almost exclusively an outgrowth of the experiences of World War II OSS officers whose equipment in many cases had been outmoded before it was put to use. The material that was available was miserably bereft of technologies that would adequately serve America's peacetime spies of the 1950s. Sending an agent radio operator on a 400-mile trek with a heavy RS-1, an equally cumbersome manually operated power generator, and a wad of cipher pads required more guts than sense. Few of these agents ever made it to where they were going, hernias taking a greater toll on CIA's human resources than alert enemy security officers.

In the mid—1950s, what Washington and most CIA field operators wanted from their agents deep in enemy territory was a faster means of getting information out to U.S. leadership. Written messages employing advanced secret writing systems, which enabled their evasion of known censorship techniques, still fell victim to the vagaries of every postal inspector from Urumchi to East Berlin. Important messages sat for days and sometimes weeks in slow mail channels. Even the still used mighty microdot, introduced by German intelligence in World War II, relied on the mail to get where it was going. The pace of information supply needed to be quickened.

In the early 1960s, the peacetime agent started getting first-generation peacetime technology. He started getting smaller, lightweight radios and more reliable batteries to power them. Now, of course, many things have changed for the better. Agent radios destined for cross-border or denied-area use have incorporated major size reduction features through advances in fashioning microcircuitry. Couple this with industry's capability to turn out lightweight polymer packaging materials and CIA is effectively sitting light-years ahead of where it was 10 years ago. Batteries for this equipment are also 100 times smaller than before and last much longer because less power is required to drive the newer sets, and the bulk of cipher packages has all but disappeared.

Science needs constantly to be set upon to keep the agency supplied with the most advanced equipment, which not only helps keep an agent alive, but assists in enabling him to continue reporting in a time-sensitive manner. Given the formidable leaps in technological advance right now, equipment invented two years ago and issued today might be outdated and dangerous for an agent to use tomorrow.

In electronic eavesdropping, virtually no experience existed prior to 1950. Starting then, CIA quickly discovered that taps of enemy phones had to be not only physically hidden, but that any radio frequency noise emanating from the target phone had to be electronically masked or buried to avoid being found by enemy audio technicians. When opposition services caught on to new signal concealment methods, CIA "elektronikers" had to make still more sophisticated adaptations.

And there was the size of the audio package to consider. In the early days, everything was too large. When assembled, CIA-tested battery assemblies (which were always more secure than electric power available in the target building), transmitters, microphones, on-and-off remote switching assemblies, and other such accoutrements could be measured in cubic feet. Electronics geniuses in and out of government attacked the problem and have now armed the agency with dozens of micro-mini electronic components that are not only more quickly and easily put in place, but render a far less decipherable spoken product for attack by opposition audio techncians, who, notwithstanding their having found a suspect signal, are effectively stymied without appropriate signal de modulation equipment in hand.

Because of the constant pressure from the field to provide equipment for or some scientific solution to a wide variety of problems, things get a bit out of whack every so often. For instance, a staff officer identified a topfloor room in a Soviet embassy where the window was open much of the year and where KGB officers gathered almost daily to plan some of their upcoming operations. The officer ventured to his superiors that

207

if he could place a small transmitter on the ledge outside that window, he would be able to supply the station and Washington with a good deal of "hot" counterintelligence. He pointed out that his most reliable support agent happened to live a mere 35 yards away, thus his apartment was ideally situated to serve as the listening post. The station and CIA headquarters were convinced, and word went out to the innovators.

About five weeks later, a scruffy little guy from northern New England reported that he had the answer, whereupon he unveiled 10 birds, each of which, on command, was purported to be able to tote a three-gram transmitter about 100 yards, lay it on a dime, and, if necessary, return for another unit.

Two weeks later, the birds were in the target capital. Right away, though, six of the birds suffered severe culture shock, or perhaps jet lag, and refused to cooperate. The other four, however, proved they were ready, willing, and able by making several successful practice runs on grounds outside the city. Everything was ready, or so everyone thought.

An after-action report was prepared two days later: "1. First of our four jonathans molting and, consequently on inactive list as his wingspan cannot sustain load for required distance.

"2. Second phoenix has become romantically involved with a ladybird in the non-cooperative six. Thus diverted and almost always exhausted, he offers indifferent response to launch commands.

"3. Third bird, having acquired a sudden and compulsively avid hunger for the transmitter, carried his package to target window, but then pecked it to pieces, and after gorging itself on the silicon/copper innards, fell into a well six storeys below, promptly disappearing without trace.

"4. Fourth bird, who throughout training has had disturbing urge to demonstrate physical prowess, did three spiral loops on way to target, then headed into the sun and over the horizon, and has not been seen since.

"5. Will advise. End of message."

So much for the "gang of four."

When the average citizen conjures up visions of a CIA staff officer working abroad, more than half of his imaginings depict the hero clandestinely photographing something. Other than the dagger and cloak, the presence of the camera always seems to get top billing. Little is known about this, but rest assured that when the CIA officer or his agent uses a camera, it hardly ever looks like a camera.

Another area of concealment involves the human agent or officer himself. There are a number of hardened professionals who, as a consequence of working many years in foreign fields, have become known to both friendly and opposition services. Nonetheless, given their linguistic talents, their hard-to-come-by area knowledge, or the inability of some of their agents to move from the sites of their assigned tasks, these individuals are required to operate in these same difficult areas where they have become targets. So ways (e. q., makeup, surgery) had to be devised to alter the operative's physical (appearance).

The key word in all this is **concealment.** Things must not appear to be what they are, or must be so small that they go unnoticed. So there is need for the magicians who can make paper, radios, liquids, and all manner of materials disappear from view. And CIA has them, those long-unsung masters of concealment who engage in the shadowiest of arts. Who are these faceless few who live on small farms in West Virginia or in the suburbs of Fredericksburg, Virginia, who say little, think much, experiment constantly, and somehow produce an item that is something other than it appears to be? They are the ever quiet men and women who make it possible for an officer to encapsulate a message for agent pick-up in a ripe tomato, and make it equally possible for the receiving agent to locate it in a warehouse or in a grocer's vegetable basket.

Richard M. Bissell, Jr. is credited with being the father of the U-2 spy plane. He also was involved in the development of sophisticated camera and satellite systems in the late 1950s and early 1960s. An economist with extensive administrative experience in government, he served as Allen Dulles's Deputy Director of Plans (now called Operations) and played a key role in planning the Bay of Pigs operation.

Q *How did you join the Central Intelligence Agency?*

A Allen Dulles recruited me from the Ford Foundation. I started February 1st, 1954. I really didn't have a formal government position. My title was Chief of Development Projects Staff.

Q *Then you became head of operations.*

A I became head, more appropriately called deputy director of plans (1958). This is now called operations.

Q *Most people remember you as the developer of the U-2. Is that what you believe has been your major contribution.*

A No. I feel more than anything else I contributed to developing the doctrine of covert action.

Q *But wasn't this started in OSS during the war?*

A Yes, it was, but I believe I advocated more of it and of a higher quality than previously developed. I mean the full range of covert action.

Q *Were the Soviets as aggressive in the 1950s as they are today in their covert action?*

A They were very aggressive and much ahead of us. They had for many years been practicing it against other countries. I tried to establish the identification of various forms of covert action that worked for us as a democracy.

Q *Was it supported?*

A Oh, yes, especially by the university community and albeit reluctantly by the State Department. The State Department began to realize diplomacy doesn't always work with Communists.

Q *Today, the debate goes on about whether covert action should be taken away from CIA and possibly eliminated or turned over to the military. How do you feel about it?*

A I know the debate is going on. It's a mistake to take it away from the CIA because clandestine collection and covert action go hand in hand and the analysis of such is an integral part. Unfortunately, most critics assume 95 percent of intelligence is covert action and 5 percent is analysis. As you know, it's the opposite. You cannot separate collection from covert action.

Q *When you ran the U-2 project, were we ahead of the Soviets?*

A Oh, yes, by many years. The U-2 was a major breakthrough for the United States. It gave us a leg up on photo reconnaissance and Soviet technological development. It was followed later by the A-11 and the SR-71.

Q *How did it contribute to the overall intelligence puzzle?*

A It enabled us to know the capabilities of Soviet bomber production and Soviet missile production. It gave us the most knowledge of Soviet bomber strength.

Q *What did the Soviets have?*

A They, of course, had satellites and although they probably stole much of our early technology regarding the U-2, they were very good in developing their own reconnaissance and missiles and satellites without copying ours. We were far ahead in optical clarity and technical interpretation. We stayed ahead for many years. It also helped us tremendously in gathering intelligence on submarine warfare.

Q *What about the state of the art and the future of technology?*

A Good question. I suspect that there will be a diminishing role of investment in money and time regarding photo reconnaissance. Satellite reconnaissance today is superb and I foresee two major things. Most reconnaissance will be by satellite platforms. It will be very hard to improve on photo intelligence. It's the best it can be right now. One can read a message printed on a fingernail from satellite cameras. The Soviets and the U.S. probably have parity. Thus, the photo aspect will be a rapidly diminishing feature of budget busters on both sides. Although we are getting into more exotic photography—radar photography, for example.

The second area I see expanding will be the whole range of listening and signals intercept from space. This, coupled with increases in submarine and underwater photography and listening, will be the technological equivalents of the U-2 in the 1960s.

Q *Who was the best Director of Central Intelligence?*

A Probably Allen Dulles. I was hired by and worked with Dulles a number of years and he was superb in building up and expanding tradecraft. But Helms, who was my deputy, has to be regarded as one of the best. He was the first professional intelligence officer. He was a paragon of the operations department and managed the expansion and professional build-up of CIA. McCone was also good, especially as an administrator.

Q *Since we are talking about operations, what was the attitude of the executive branch. Eisenhower, Kennedy, and Johnson all advocated and supported aggressive operations and covert action.*

A That's true, and all realized that we had to be in the game since the Soviets were conducting so many active measures and operations against the West. During the Kennedy years, John Kennedy delegated the attorney general to monitor and push CIA operations. He was like a case officer during Operation Mongoose and spent a lot of time being involved in the details of the covert action.

Q *Who are the people that stand out for you in the CIA?*

A Frank Wisner—creative and constructive director of operations, pulled the clandestine service together. James Angleton—brilliant, one-of-a-kind master of counterintelligence. Cord Meyer—a creator of special covert operations, through international groups, labor unions, authors, publishers. John Bross—Deputy Director, expert on German Operations. Desmond FitzGerald —a dashing Irishman and an excellent covert operator. William King Harvey—a cowboy, but a good operator in his early career. Richard Helms—a real professional, the best the CIA had.

Sherman Kent—Board of Estimats and supporter of CIA. Sheffield Edwards—head of all security; that's why CIA was never penetrated. Lyman Kirkpatrick—ambitious and an important figure in the 1950s.

Q *Do you think the world would have been different without a CIA.*

A If you look at the number of successes we have had, definitely.

Q *How is the CIA uniquely American, especially compared to foreign agencies?*

A Well, for one thing, even in covert operations, a person's life was always prized. Yes, we were embarrassed by the U-2, but we got Gary Powers back alive. Yes, the Carter administration was castigated by the hostage situation, but we got the hostages safely back. There are a number of instances like this. People also forget that we had a very fine legal staff that gave us advice on what was constitutionally allowed, and that most plans were approved or initiated by the President and on the whole supported by members of Congress, the State Department, and the military.

Q *Do you agree the CIA has a bad name within the American public's view?*

A Oh, yes. That's because we never had good public relations. The FBI under J. Edgar Hoover always had good public relations. The early CIA people felt it wasn't necessary because everything could be kept secure and secret. In a democracy that's tough to do.

At left is a publication of the National Intelligence Study Center an educational organization promoting accurate information about intelligence and the CIA. At the left is the Foreign Intelligence Literary Scene by Thomas Troy a former CIA staffer who covers the literary scene on intelligence.

The Glomar Explorer project was an engineering masterpiece. It helped raise part of a submerged Soviet submarine.

The word *clandestine* denotes stealth. A clandestine service is, clearly, designed to use stealth on behalf of its government. Stealth is, to most of us, an unattractive concept, except when it is practiced by young lovers. Yet organized societies have used it against each other as long as the affairs of mankind have been recorded. All modern nations—democratic no less than totalitarian—with foreign interests have felt obliged to sponsor some form of clandestine activity, although most do not, as a rule, officially acknowledge this.

Totalitarian countries foster a way of life and government compatible with clandestine action. In democratic societies, clandestinity is not as easily reconciled with the principles of open government, but it is no less necessary to the conduct of foreign affairs. The case was succinctly articulated by former CIA Director Richard Helms: "This is neither a boy scout game nor a boxing bout fought by the Marquess of Queensberry rules. It's a job to be done."

The "job to be done" falls into two broad categories: (1) espionage (and counterespionage)—the collection of information by surreptitious means, and (2) covert action—surreptitious actions in support of American policy objectives abroad. Espionage is needed to collect information required for policy-making, analysis, and security. Covert action is meant to influence people and events abroad, as deemed desirable by our policymakers. The principal similarity is that both espionage and covert action rely on unconventional methods and secrecy.

Espionage

Boiled down to its simplest form, espionage is a system for satisfying our government's requirements—actual, implied, or anticipated—for significant information not otherwise available. The last three words are important. Many agencies and many official and private observers report significant information that keeps the government abreast of foreign trends and events. No clandestine means are needed to gather this information, so none are used. Where government needs can be met through other channels, it makes no sense to mobilize clandestine resources, for their use is riskier, costlier, and potentially more troublesome.

CIA officers training Tibetan troops . . . in Colorado.

But often the risk, cost, and potential for trouble are unavoidable. For example, a nation that has no diplomatic relations with the United States is conducting large-scale maneuvers close to the border of one of our small allies, and our government needs to know whether or not the exercises are a cover for actual aggression. Or a number of Americans traveling abroad have mysteriously disappeared, but the country in which they were traveling denies any knowledge of the Americans' whereabouts. Clandestine inquiries may provide the only chance to establish the truth in these cases.

These examples show the rationale for clandestine collection missions, not their range or orientation. Their range is nearly as wide and varied as the foreign interests of our nation. Their orientation is governed by worldwide relationships and potential threats. Many elements, like American-Soviet relations, require continuing attention. Others, like terrorist threats, are recurrent. And many other needs arise from unanticipated developments.

What are those clandestine means employed to serve American requirements? For one, there are technical devices—photographic, electronic, and acoustic. After what now looks like crude beginnings, they have become increasingly sophisticated, and their use has been emphasized in recent years. But the essence of clandestine operations has been and remains the human agent, who can not only see physical evidence but, at his best, can ascertain the disposition and intent of those whose resources and influence make them subjects of our concern. The selection, recruitment, maintenance, testing, and protection of human agents willing and in a position to help us where help is needed are sensitive and immensely complicated tasks, for the motivations, needs, and vulnerabilities of such individuals cover the spectrum of human nature and circumstance. The job is made still more complex by the need to maintain proper standards of accuracy and timeliness for the information such agents supply, because not all are equally perceptive, reliable, or well placed. In each case, the value and potential of the agent and the operation must be correlated with the risk in running them. Depending on the circumstances, an exposed agent may lose his standing, his livelihood, his freedom, or even his life.

Despite all the difficulties, the Clandestine Service has over the years, and through the vagaries of changing times, managed to acquire and maintain an impressive array of reliable agents. Experiences collected over time have been distilled into operating doctrine and methodology, and in that form have been passed on to young officers entering the Clan-

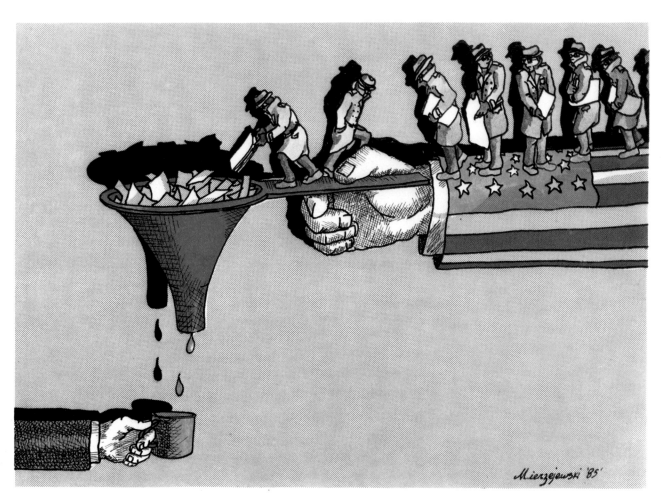

Mierzejewski '85

destine Service. Thus, institutional memory has been preserved.

In passing, it might be noted that in practice human agents and technical devices are, of course, not kept separate from each other.

Counterespionage, or counterintelligence, is related to other collection activities because it, too, is designed to collect information and because it relies on the same data base and methodology. But the information required for counterespionage purposes pertains primarily to foreign, essentially adversary intelligence services: how they operate, what they are doing or planning to do, and what they are trying to find out about us. All this is peripheral to the main task: the discovery and abortion of attempts by foreign powers to penetrate our government institutions.

This work, directed against skilled adversaries, is especially sensitive, because even a minor lapse could thwart a major effort. Painstaking attention to detail is required, along with caution and skepticism. It is, more than anything else, a job for professionals.

Covert Action

Covert action, more recently called *special activities*—that is, activities designed to influence people and events abroad in line with American policy objectives—at one time commanded the lion's share of the Clandestine Service's budget. But that ratio

changed a long time ago. Nevertheless, public attention has been drawn to covert action more than to anything else, presumably because some major undertakings exploded into headlines and gave rise to widespread criticism. But aside from the merits or demerits of specific operations, covert action has retained recognition as an indispensable instrument of American foreign policy. Sometimes it offers the only viable choice between open intervention, perhaps at the risk of armed conflict, and letting our adversaries have their way.

The most prevalent form of covert action is political. This type of action, though usually the response to significant developments, has actually been invoked most often in a limited context and on a small scale. Advantage has been taken of various opportunities to present pro-American views, for instance, or to dispute anti-American statements. This kind of promotion has carried little risk and provoked less controversy.

But there is another major area of covert action, known as paramilitary operations. They are really military campaigns, covert only in the sense that the national sponsorship remains unacknowledged, often by tacit agreement on both sides. They lie outside the pattern of other clandestine operations, because little about them can be concealed.

Implicit in the foregoing and worth stating explicitly is that the Clandestine Service is charged with

BOOK OF HONOR

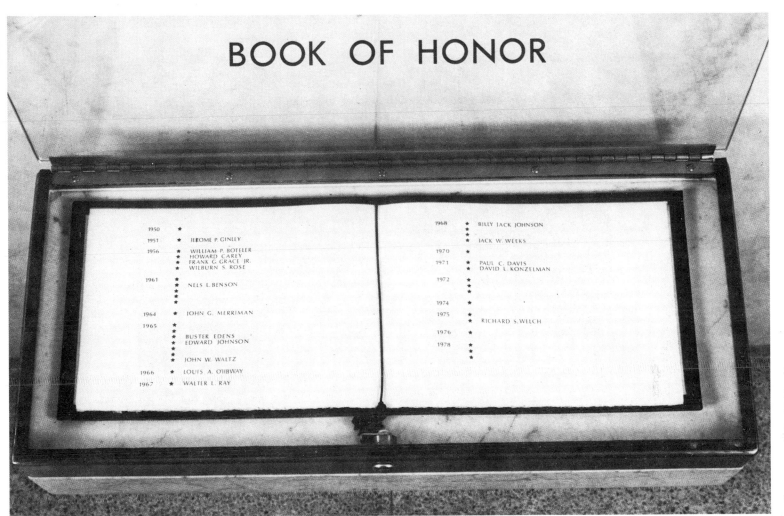

1950	★	
1951	★	JEROME P. GINLEY
1956	★	WILLIAM P. BOTELER
	★	HOWARD CAREY
	★	FRANK G. GRACE JR.
	★	WILBURN S. ROSE
1961	★	
	★	NELS L. BENSON
	★	
	★	
	★	
	★	
1964	★	JOHN G. MERRIMAN
1965	★	
	★	
	★	BUSTER EDENS
	★	EDWARD JOHNSON
	★	
	★	JOHN W. WALTZ
1966	★	LOUIS A. OJIBWAY
1967	★	WALTER L. RAY

1968	★	BILLY JACK JOHNSON
	★	
	★	JACK W. WEEKS
1970	★	
1971	★	PAUL C. DAVIS
	★	DAVID L. KONZELMAN
1972	★	
	★	
	★	
1974	★	
1975	★	
	★	RICHARD S. WELCH
1976	★	
1978	★	
	★	

executing covert action policy, not with designing it. The policy is defined by the President and implemented by the responsible members of his official family. Many people add their voices along the way. Speaking of Clandestine Service or CIA "policy" in this area is comparable to holding the police responsible for the content of criminal law.

The Clandestine Service is a thoroughly American institution, and it forswears neither fair play nor free expression. But there is a need for adaptation; particularly, one has to learn to share professional problems with professional colleagues, not with the world at large, and to keep one's friends and neighbors in the dark about one's daily activities. The work offers its practitioners a mixture of self-denial and distinction, of limitation and security, of insulation and assurance. The appeal is essentially that of patriotism, trust, predictability, and belonging. Basic standards and priorities are clear and their protection and acceptance rarely questioned.

A good part of that tradition survives, but the structure has been jarred by a number of shocks. It held up under the reverberations of the abortive Bay of Pigs landing (1961) and the disclosure of secret subsidies for American student groups (1967). It survived the Watergate scandal and the subsequent barrage of media and public criticism in the early and mid-1970s. But the scale of the assault was unprecedented, and its effect on the daily life, effectiveness, and outlook of the Clandestine Service and its officers was profound. One-time secrets were prominently exposed, past and long-corrected errors and trespasses were magnified, unconventional actions were measured by the standards of civic virtue, and the service was blamed for having followed directions now deemed unpopular. Pride turned to dismay, daring to caution, certainty to doubt.

Under CIA Director William J. Casey, the Clandestine Service, along with the rest of the organization, has found new levels of support and invigoration. Obviously external conditions, including the existence of jurisdiction-conscious congressional intelligence committees and the emergence of more assertive and less inhibited media critics, would make it impossible to return to the insulation of pre-Watergate days, even if it was desirable. Covert action planners, in particular, will probably continue to work under a handicap, and mishaps like the Vitaly Yurchenko redefection are likely to get a full public airing. But fundamentally, one senses that the nation is accepting the Clandestine Service as an asset and a necessity. This acceptance will provide a solid foundation on which Casey and future directors may build.

SIDNEY WILIAM SOUERS

(Portrait by C. L. MacNelly)

DIRECTORS OF CENTRAL INTELLIGENCE

SIDNEY WILLIAM SOUERS

Rear Admiral, U.S. Naval Reserve

TENURE AS DCI	23 January 1946–10 June 1946
BIRTH	30 March 1892, Dayton, Ohio
EDUCATION	Attended Purdue University; Miami University (Ohio), B.A., 1914
APPOINTMENT	Appointed by President Harry S. Truman and sworn in on 23 January 1946 [1]
RELIEVED	Resigned, effective 10 June 1946
DEPUTY DIRECTOR	Kingman Douglass (Acting)
EARLIER CAREER	Private business
	Commissioned Lieutenant Commander in the U.S. Naval Reserve, 1929
	Volunteered for active duty, July 1940
	Promoted to Rear Admiral and made Deputy Chief of Naval Intelligence, 1945
LATER CAREER	Executive Secretary of the National Security Council, 26 September 1947–15 January 1950
	Returned to private business
	Died 14 January 1973

(Portrait by C. L. MacNelly)

HOYT SANFORD VANDENBERG

HOYT SANFORD VANDENBERG

Lieutenant General, U.S. Army (Army Air Forces)

TENURE AS DCI   10 June 1946–1 May 1947

BIRTH   24 January 1899, Milwaukee, Wisconsin

EDUCATION   Graduated U.S. Military Academy, 1923; Army War College, 1936

APPOINTMENT   Appointed by President Harry S. Truman, 7 June 1946; sworn in 10 June 1946 [1]

RELIEVED   Reassigned as Deputy Commander, U.S. Army Air Forces, 1 May 1947

DEPUTY DIRECTOR   Kingman Douglass (Acting) until 11 July 1946; Brigadier General Edwin Kennedy Wright, U.S. Army, from 20 January 1947 for remainder of tenure

EARLIER CAREER   Commanded 9th Air Force in Europe during World War II

Assistant Chief of Staff, G-2, War Department General Staff, January–June 1946

LATER CAREER   Appointed Vice Chief of Staff of U.S. Air Force with rank of General, U.S. Air Force, effective 1 October 1947

Chief of Staff, U.S. Air Force, 1948–1953

Retired from Air Force and Joint Chiefs of Staff, 30 June 1953

Died 2 April 1954

(Portrait by Comis)

ROSCOE HENRY HILLENKOETTER

ROSCOE HENRY HILLENKOETTER

Rear Admiral, U.S. Navy

TENURE AS DCI	1 May 1947–7 October 1950
BIRTH	8 May 1897, St. Louis, Missouri
EDUCATION	Graduated U.S. Naval Academy, 1919 (Class of 1920)
APPOINTMENT	Appointed by President Harry S. Truman, 30 April 1947; sworn in 1 May 1947
	Recess appointment under new law, 29 August 1947; sworn in 26 September 1947
	Reappointed under new law by President Harry S. Truman, 24 November 1947 and confirmed by U.S. Senate, 8 December 1947
RELIEVED	Returned to Navy sea command, 7 October 1950
DEPUTY DIRECTOR	Brigadier General Edwin Kennedy Wright until 9 March 1949
EARLIER CAREER	Several tours as Assistant Naval Attaché or Naval Attaché, France, 1933–1935, 1938–1940, 1940–1941 (Vichy), and 1946–1947
	Officer in Charge of Intelligence, on the staff of Commander in Chief, Pacific Ocean Area (Admiral Chester W. Nimitz), September 1942–March 1943
	Promoted to Rear Admiral, 29 November 1946
LATER CAREER	Commander, Navy Task Force in the Korean War, November 1950–September 1951
	Promoted to Vice Admiral, 9 April 1956
	Inspector General of the Navy, 1 August 1956
	Retired from Navy, 1 May 1957
	Private business
	Died 18 June 1982

(Portrait by , F. Draper)

WALTER BEDELL SMITH

WALTER BEDELL SMITH

General, U.S. Army

TENURE AS DCI	7 October 1950–9 February 1953
BIRTH	5 October 1895, Indianapolis, Indiana
EDUCATION	Attended Butler University briefly
APPOINTMENT	Appointed by President Harry S. Truman, 21 August 1950
	Confirmed by U.S. Senate, 28 August 1950
	Sworn in, 7 October 1950
	Promoted to General, U.S. Army, effective 1 August 1951
RELIEVED	Resigned to become Under Secretary of State, 9 February 1953
DEPUTY DIRECTOR	William H. Jackson October 1950–August 1951; Allen W. Dulles for remainder of tenure
EARLIER CAREER	During World War II served as Chief of Staff of the Allied Forces in North Africa and the Mediterranean, and then as Chief of Staff to General Eisenhower, Supreme Headquarters, Allied Expeditionary Forces
	Promoted to Lieutenant General, 13 January 1944
	U.S. Ambassador to the Soviet Union, 1946–1949
	Commanding General of the First Army, 1949–1950
LATER CAREER	Retired from Army, 9 February 1953
	Private business
	Died 9 August 1961

ALLEN WELSH DULLES

226

ALLEN WELSH DULLES

TENURE AS DCI	26 February 1953–29 November 1961
BIRTH	7 April 1893, Watertown, New York
EDUCATION	Princeton University, B.A., 1914, M.A., 1916; George Washington University, LL.B., 1926
APPOINTMENT	Appointed by President Dwight D. Eisenhower, 10 February 1953 (served as Acting Director pending confirmation)
	Confirmed by U.S. Senate, 23 February 1953
	Sworn in, 26 February 1953
	Requested by President-elect John F. Kennedy to continue as Director of Central Intelligence, 10 November 1960
RELIEVED	Retired, 29 November 1961
DEPUTY DIRECTOR	General Charles Pearre Cabell, U.S. Air Force
EARLIER CAREER	U.S. Diplomatic Service, Department of State, 1916–1926
	Practiced law in New York, 1926–1942 and 1946–1950
	Head of Office of Strategic Services' office in Berne, Switzerland, 1942–1945
	Previous service in CIA as Deputy Director for Plans, December 1950–August 1951, and Deputy Director of Central Intelligence, 23 August 1951–26 February 1953
LATER CAREER	Retired to private life and writing
	Served on President's Commission on the Assassination of President Kennedy, 1963–1964
	Died 28 January 1969

JOHN ALEX McCONE

(Portrait by William F. Draper)

JOHN ALEX McCONE

TENURE AS DCI	29 November 1961–28 April 1965
BIRTH	4 January 1902, San Francisco, California
EDUCATION	Attended University of California
APPOINTMENT	Appointed by President John F. Kennedy, 27 September 1961
	Sworn in as recess appointee, 29 November 1961
	Confirmed by U.S. Senate, 31 January 1962
RELIEVED	Resigned, effective 28 April 1965
DEPUTY DIRECTOR	Lieutenant General Marshall A. Carter, U.S. Army
EARLIER CAREER	Private business
	Member of President's Air Policy Commission, 1947–1948
	Deputy to the Secretary of Defense, March–November 1948
	Under Secretary of the Air Force, 1950–1951
	Chairman, Atomic Energy Commission, 1958–1960
LATER CAREER	Private business
	Counselor to the President's Commission on Strategic Forces, 1983

(Portrait by Rudolf A. Bernatschke)

WILLIAM FRANCIS RABORN, Jr.

WILLIAM FRANCIS RABORN, Jr.

Vice Admiral, U.S. Navy (Retired)

TENURE AS DCI	28 April 1965–30 June 1966
BIRTH	8 June 1905, Decatur, Texas
EDUCATION	Graduated U.S. Naval Academy, 1928; Naval War College, 1952
APPOINTMENT	Appointed by President Lyndon B. Johnson, 11 April 1965
	Confirmed by U.S. Senate, 22 April 1965
	Sworn in, 28 April 1965
RELIEVED	Resigned, 30 June 1966
DEPUTY DIRECTOR	Richard M. Helms
EARLIER CAREER	Director, Special Projects Office, U.S. Navy (developed Polaris missile for Fleet Ballistic Missile System) 1955–1962
	Deputy Chief of Naval Operations (Development), 1962–1963
	Retired from Navy, 1 September 1963
	Private industry, 1963–1965
LATER CAREER	Private business

RICHARD McGARRAH HELMS

(Portrait by William F. Draper)

RICHARD McGARRAH HELMS

TENURE AS DCI	30 June 1966–2 February 1973
BIRTH	30 March 1913, St. Davids, Pennsylvania
EDUCATION	Williams College, B.A., 1935
APPOINTMENT	Appointed by President Lyndon B. Johnson, 18 June 1966
	Confirmed by U.S. Senate, 28 June 1966
	Sworn in, 30 June 1966
RELIEVED	Retired, 2 February 1973
DEPUTY DIRECTOR	Vice Admiral Rufus L. Taylor, U.S. Navy, 13 October 1966–31 January 1969; Lieutenant General Robert E. Cushman, Jr., U.S. Marine Corps, 7 May 1969–31 December 1971; Lieutenant General Vernon A. Walters, U.S. Army, 2 May 1972 for remainder of tenure
EARLIER CAREER	Journalist
	Commissioned into U.S. Naval Reserve, 1942
	Served with Office of Strategic Services and its successors, 1943–1946
	Career in CIA
	Deputy Director for Plans, 1962–1965
	Deputy Director of Central Intelligence, 28 April 1965–30 June 1966
LATER CAREER	Ambassador to Iran, March 1973–January 1977
	Private consultant since 1977
	Member of President's Commission on Strategic Forces, 1983

JAMES RODNEY SCHLESINGER

JAMES RODNEY SCHLESINGER

TENURE AS DCI	2 February 1973–2 July 1973
BIRTH	15 February 1929, New York, New York
EDUCATION	Harvard University, A.B., 1950, A.M., 1952 and Ph.D., 1956
APPOINTMENT	Appointed by President Richard M. Nixon, 21 December 1972
	Confirmed by U.S. Senate, 23 January 1973
	Sworn in, 2 February 1973
RELIEVED	Resigned, effective 2 July 1973, to become Secretary of Defense
DEPUTY DIRECTOR	Lieutenant General Vernon A. Walters, U.S. Army [1]
EARLIER CAREER	Assistant and Associate Professor of Economics, University of Virginia, 1955–1963
	Rand Corporation, Senior Staff Member, 1963–1967; Director of Strategic Studies, 1967–1969
	Assistant Director and Acting Deputy Director, Bureau of the Budget, 1969–1970
	Assistant Director, Office of Management and Budget, 1970–1971
	Chairman, Atomic Energy Commission, 1971–1973
LATER CAREER	Secretary of Defense, 1973–1975
	Secretary of Energy, 1977–1979
	Private consultant since 1979
	Counselor to the President's Commission on Strategic Forces, 1983

WILLIAM EGAN COLBY

WILLIAM EGAN COLBY

TENURE AS DCI	4 September 1973–30 January 1976
BIRTH	4 January 1920, St. Paul, Minnesota
EDUCATION	Princeton University, B.A., 1940; Columbia University, LL.B., 1947
APPOINTMENT	Appointed by President Richard M. Nixon, 10 May 1973
	Confirmed by U.S. Senate, 1 August 1973
	Sworn in, 4 September 1973
RELIEVED	Retired, 30 January 1976
DEPUTY DIRECTOR	Lieutenant General Vernon A. Walters, U.S. Army
EARLIER CAREER	Commissioned into U.S. Army, August 1941
	Served with Office of Strategic Services, 1943–1945
	Attorney in private practice, New York, 1947–1949; with National Labor Relations Board, Washington, D.C., 1949–1950
	Career in CIA
	Chief, Far East Division, 1962–1967
	On leave from CIA, assigned to Agency for International Development as Director of Civil Operations and Rural Development Support, Saigon (with rank of Ambassador), 1968–1971
	Executive Director-Comptroller, 1972–1973
	Deputy Director for Operations, 1973
LATER CAREER	Private law practice

(Portrait by C. L. MacNelly)

GEORGE HERBERT WALKER BUSH

238

GEORGE HERBERT WALKER BUSH

TENURE AS DCI	30 January 1976–20 January 1977
BIRTH	12 June 1924, Milton, Massachusetts
EDUCATION	Yale University, B.A., 1948
APPOINTMENT	Appointed by President Gerald R. Ford, 3 November 1975
	Confirmed by U.S. Senate, 27 January 1976
	Sworn in, 30 January 1976
RELIEVED	Resigned, 20 January 1977
DEPUTY DIRECTOR	Lieutenant General Vernon A. Walters, U.S. Army, until 2 July 1976; E. Henry Knoche for remainder of tenure
EARLIER CAREER	Served in World War II as naval aviator in the Pacific
	Private business
	Member of Congress, 7th District, Texas, 1966–1970
	Ambassador to the United Nations, 1971–1972
	Chairman, Republican National Committee, 1973–1974
	Chief, U.S. Liaison Office, People's Republic of China, 1974–1975
LATER CAREER	Private business and politics
	Sworn in as Vice President of the United States, 20 January 1981

STANSFIELD TURNER

(Portrait by William F. Draper)

STANSFIELD TURNER

Admiral, U.S. Navy (Retired)

TENURE AS DCI	9 March 1977–20 January 1981
BIRTH	1 December 1923, Highland Park, Illinois
EDUCATION	Attended Amherst College, 1941–1943; graduated U.S. Naval Academy, 1946 (Class of 1947); Rhodes Scholar, Oxford University, B.A., 1950, M.A., 1954
APPOINTMENT	Appointed by President Jimmy Carter, 8 February 1977
	Confirmed by U.S. Senate, 24 February 1977
	Sworn in, 9 March 1977
	Retired from active duty in U.S. Navy, 31 December 1978
RELIEVED	Resigned, 20 January 1981
DEPUTY DIRECTOR	E. Henry Knoche, until 1 August 1977; Frank C. Carlucci for remainder of tenure
EARLIER CAREER	Director, Systems Analysis Division, Office of the Chief of Naval Operations, 1971–1972
	Promoted to Vice Admiral, 1972
	President, U.S. Naval War College, 1972–1974
	Commander, U.S. Second Fleet, 1974–1975
	Promoted to Admiral, 1975
	Commander-in-Chief, Allied Forces, Southern Europe (NATO), 1975–1977
LATER CAREER	Private consulting and writing

WILLIAM JOSEPH CASEY

(Photograph by Everett Raymond Kinstler)

WILLIAM JOSEPH CASEY

TENURE AS DCI	Since 28 January 1981
BIRTH	13 March 1913, New York, New York
EDUCATION	Fordham University, B.S., 1934; St. John's University, LL.B., 1937
APPOINTMENT	Appointed by President Ronald Reagan, 13 January 1981
	Confirmed by U.S. Senate, 27 January 1981
	Sworn in, 28 January 1981
DEPUTY DIRECTOR	Admiral Bobby Ray Inman, U.S. Navy, 12 February 1981–10 June 1982, and John N. McMahon from 10 June 1982
EARLIER CAREER	Lawyer and businessman
	Commissioned into U.S. Naval Reserve, 1943
	Wartime service with Office of Strategic Services, becoming Chief of the Special Intelligence Branch in European Theater of Operations, 1944
	Associate General Counsel at the European Headquarters of the Marshall Plan, 1948
	Chairman of the Securities and Exchange Commission, 1971–1973
	Under Secretary of State for Economic Affairs, 1973–1974
	President and Chairman of the Export-Import Bank of the United States, 1974–1976
	Member, President's Foreign Intelligence Advisory Board, 1976–1977
	Campaign Manager for Ronald Reagan, 1980

CIA MEDALS

DISTINGUISHED INTELLIGENCE CROSS

For a voluntary act or acts of exceptional heroism involving the acceptance of existing dangers with conspicuous fortitude and exemplary courage.

DISTINGUISHED INTELLIGENCE MEDAL

For performance of outstanding services or for achievement of a distinctly exceptional nature in a duty or responsibility.

INTELLIGENCE STAR

For a voluntary act or acts of courage performed under hazardous conditions or for outstanding achievements or services rendered with distinction under conditions of grave risk.

INTELLIGENCE MEDAL OF MERIT

For the performance of especially meritorious service or for an act or achievement conspicuously above normal duties.

CAREER INTELLIGENCE MEDAL

For a cumulative record of service which reflects exceptional achievement.

INTELLIGENCE COMMENDATION MEDAL

For the performance of especially commendable service or for an act or achievement significantly above normal duties which results in an important contribution to the mission of the Agency.

EXCEPTIONAL SERVICE MEDALLION

For injury or death resulting from service in an area of hazard.

SILVER RETIREMENT MEDALLION

For a career of 25 years or more with the Agency.

BRONZE RETIREMENT MEDALLION

For a career of at least 15 but less than 25 years with the Agency.

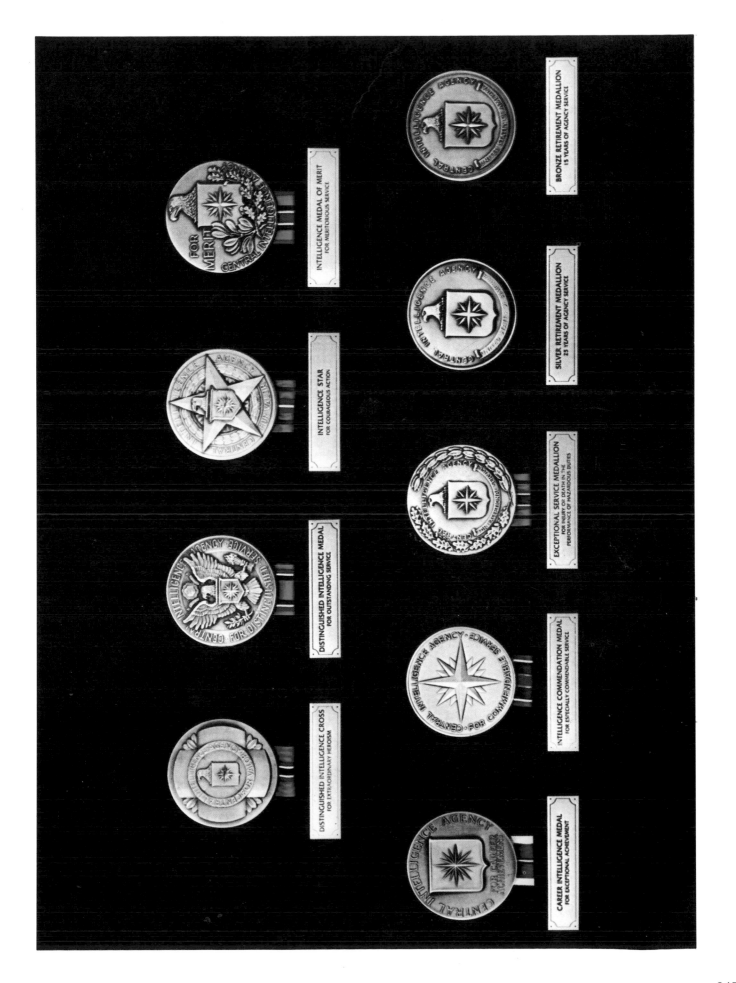

INTELLIGENCE MEDAL OF MERIT
FOR MERITORIOUS SERVICE

BRONZE RETIREMENT MEDALLION
15 YEARS OF AGENCY SERVICE

INTELLIGENCE STAR
FOR COURAGEOUS ACTION

SILVER RETIREMENT MEDALLION
25 YEARS OF AGENCY SERVICE

DISTINGUISHED INTELLIGENCE MEDAL
FOR OUTSTANDING SERVICE

EXCEPTIONAL SERVICE MEDALLION
FOR INJURY OR DEATH IN THE
PERFORMANCE OF HAZARDOUS DUTIES

DISTINGUISHED INTELLIGENCE CROSS
FOR EXTRAORDINARY HEROISM

INTELLIGENCE COMMENDATION MEDAL
FOR ESPECIALLY COMMENDABLE SERVICE

CAREER INTELLIGENCE MEDAL
FOR EXCEPTIONAL ACHIEVEMENT

Richard K. Betts—Senior fellow in foreign policy studies, Brookings Institution. Served in staffs, Senate Select Committee on Intelligence and National Security Council; professor and lecturer, Harvard, Columbia, Johns Hopkins, National War College, et al. Author of **Soldiers, Statesmen, and Cold War Crises** (1977), et el.; winner of awards from National Intelligence Study Center for articles, 1979, 1981.

Richard M. Bissell, Jr. — Management consultant. Special assistant to CIA Director, 1954—59, Deputy Director, Plans, 1959—62; Director of Marketing and Economic Planning, United Aircraft Corp. Recipient, National Security Medal, 1962.

Scott D. Breckinridge — Guest lecturer, University of Kentucky; semiretired from CIA. Served in CIA Inspector General's office, including six years as Depoty Inspector General; practiced law before joining CIA. Author of **The CIA and the U.S. Intelligence System** (1986). Twice recipient, Distinguished Inteligence Medal.

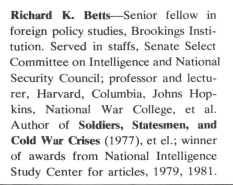

Marjorie W. Cline — Vice-President, SIFT, Inc. (private foreign affairs research corporation). Research editor, National Geographic Society Special Publications Series; writer and editor, **China Letter** (bimonthly newsletter on China and Taiwan). Author of **Teaching Intelligence in the Mid-1980s** (1984); edited **Scholar's Guide to Intelligence Literature** (1983), et al.

Ray S. Cline — Senior advisor, Center for Strategic and International Studies, adjunct professor, School of Foreign Service, Georgetown University. Served in OSS; CIA officer and chief of station, Deputy Director for Intelligence, 1962—66; Director, Bureau of Intelligence and Research, 1969—73. Author of **The CIA under Reagan, Bush, and Casey** (1981), et al.

William E. Colby — International consultant. OSS service in France and Norway; CIA, 1950—76, including chief of Far East Divison (1962—68), Executive Director Comptroller (1972—73), Director of Central Intelligence (1973—76). Author of **Honorable Men: My Life in the CIA** (1978), et al.

Joseph C. Goulden — Writer. Author of **Truth Is the First Casualty** (1969), **The Death Merchant** (1984), et al. Served in army counterintelligence corps; worked as newspaperman, including Washington bureau chief, **Philadelphia Inquirer,** before turning to books, of which he has written 14 nonfiction titles.

Morton H. Halperin — Director, Washington office of the American Civil Liberties Union, and Center for National Security Studies; critic of CIA and government abuses. Deputy Assistant Secretary of Defense; senior staff member, National Security Council; senior fellow, Brookings Institution; professor of government, Harvard. Author of **Bureaucratic Politics and Foreign Policy** (1974), et al.

Samuel Halpern — Consultant on intelligence and national security. Thirty-two-year veteran of OSS and CIA; serves or has served on boards of directors of Association of Former Intelligence Officers, National Intelligence Study Center, et al. Author of "Clandestine Collection," in **Intelligence Requirements for the 1980s: Elements of Intelligence** (ed. Roy Godson, 1983), et al.

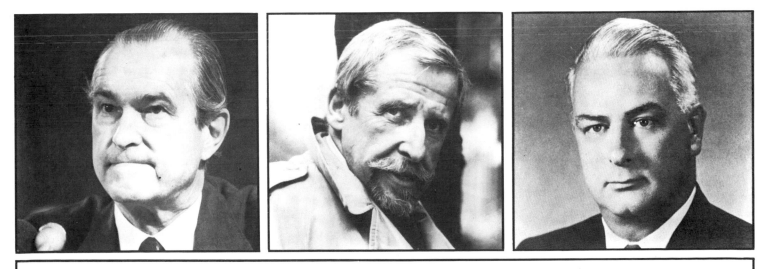

Richard M. Helms — International consultant. Served in CIA, 1947—73, including Deputy Director (1965—66), Director of Central Intelligence (1966—73); U.S. ambassador to Iran, 1973—76).

William Hood — Writer. Author of **Mole** (1982), **Spy Wednesday,** (1986), et al. Worked for **Portland** (Maine) **Press Herald;** Military Intelligence Service and OSS; CIA officer until 1975.

Lyman B. Kirkpatrick, Jr. — Educator. Served in OSS; CIA officer, 1947—65, including Inspector General (1953—61), Executive Director (1962—65); professor, Brown University, Havy War College. Author of **The Real CIA** (1968), **The U. S. Intelligence Community: Foreign Policy and Domestic Activities** (1969), et al. Recipient of numerous awards, including the Distinguished Intelligence Medal, 1965.

Cord Meyer — Syndicated columnist. CIA officer, 1951—77, including Assistant Deputy Director, Plans (1967—73), chief of station, London (1973—76); lecturer, Georgetown University, 1982—85. Author of **Facing Reality** (1980), et al. Three times recipient, Distinguished Intelligence Medal.

Hans Moses — Editor, researcher. Worked for U. S. Army and Air Force intelligence; CIA Clandestine Service officer, 1953—74. Author of **The Clandestine Service of the Central Intelligence Agency** (1983), et al.

Walter L. Pforzheimer — Attorney, consultant, adjunct professor at the Defense Intelligence College. CIG/CIA, 1946—74, including legislative counsel (1946—56); established CIA Historical Intelligence Collection, 1956; consultant to CIA general counsel, 1974—77; President-elect Reagan's CIA Transition Team, 1980—81.

David Atlee Phillips — Writer, lecturer, CIA officer, 1950—75, including chief of Latin American operations; founder, Association of Former Intelligence Officers and CHALLENGE, an intelligence officers' legal action fund. Author of **The Night Watch: 25 Years of Peculiar Service** (1977), **Careers in Secret Operations** (1984), et al.

Thomas Polgar — Management consultant, writer. CIA career officer, including chief of station; consultant to Defense Intelligence Agency and to commercial interests in the United States, Europe, and Latin America. Recipient of numerous awards, including the Intelligence Star and two Distinguished Intelligence Medals. Author of **The KGB: An Instrument of Soviet Power,** et al.

Thomas Powers — Writer. Author of **Diana: The Making of a Terrorist** (1971), **The Man Who Kept the Secrets: Richard Helms and the CIA** (1979), et al., numerous articles published in **The Atlantic, Harper's, The New York Review of Books,** et al. Journalist for **Rome** (Italy) **Daily American,** 1965—67, United Press International, New York, 1967—70. Recipient of Pulitzer Prize for national reporting, 1971; National Intelligence Study Center book award, 1980.

Harry Howe Ransom — Professor of political science, Vanderbilt University. Taught at Vassar, Princeton, Michigan State, and Harvard, where he co-organized the Defense Studies Program. Author of **Central Intelligence and National Security** (1958), **The Intelligence Establishment** (1970), et al.

Harry A. Rositzke — Writer, lecturer, farmer. Author of **The CIA's Secret Operations** (1977), **The KGB: The Eyes of Russia** (1981), et al.; numerous articles published in **New York Times, Washington Post,** et al. Professor, University of Omaha, Harvard, University of Rochester, 1935—42; OSS, 1944—46; CIG/CIA officer, 1946—70, including Chief of Soviet Operations (1946—52).

Lawrence B. Sulc — President, Nathan Hale Foundation and Nathan Hale Institute. CIA operations officer, 23 years; aide to U.S. House of Representatives Committee on Foreign Relations; Deputy Assistant Secretary for Interdepartmental Affairs, Bureau of Intelligence and Research. Author of "Active Measures, Quiet War, and Two Socialist Revolutions."

Thomas F. Troy — Writer, editor, Author of **Donovan and the CIA** (1981), edited **Grave Things: The OSS Journal of James Grafton Rogers** (1986), et al. Thirty year veteran of CIA. Founding editor of **Foreign Intelligence Literary Scene** (newsletter).

Stansfield Turner — Writer, lecturer. Author of **Secrecy and Democracy** (1985). U. S. Navy Admiral; president, Navy War College, 1972—74; Commander in Chief, NATO Southern Flank, 1975—77; Director of Central Intelligence, 1977—81. Recipient, National Security Medal, 1981.

John S. Warner — Retired CIA officer and U. S. Air Force Reserve major general. Served in OSS; CIA officer, 1947—76, including legislative counsel, deputy general counsel, and general counsel; legal advisor and board member, Association of Former Intelligence Officers. Author of "National Security and the First Amendment," in **The First Amendment and National Security** (ed. Paul Stephen, 1984), et al.

PFIAB

The President's Foreign Intelligence Advisory Board (PFIAB) serves for two-year terms. The board was reconstituted by the President on October 28, 1985, by Executive Order 12537. The most significant change in the new board is that it establishes a limit of 14 members.

The PFIAB is a permanent, nonpartisan body of distinguished Americans who perform a continuing and objective review of the performance of the intelligence community. The board reports directly to the President and has full access to all information necessary to advise the President on the conduct, management, and coordination of the various agencies of the intelligence community.

The PFIAB (originally known as the Board of Consultants on Foreign Intelligence Activities) was first established by President Eisenhower in 1956. The board was continued by each President thereafter until its termination in 1977 by President Carter. The PFIAB was re-formed by President Reagan on October 20, 1981, by Executive Order 12331.

On the new board, Anne Armstrong will serve as chairwoman and Leo Cherne as vice-chairman.

The following (the first 10 reappointees and the final 4 new appointees) are the members who will serve on the new board:

ANNE LEGENDRE ARMSTRONG is currently chairwoman of the Advisory Board of the Georgetown University Center for Strategic and International Studies. She was United States ambassador to Great Britain in 1976–77, and served as counsellor to the President in 1973–74. She is married, has five children, and resides in Armstrong, Texas.

LEO CHERNE is an economist and currently serves as executive director of the Research Institute of America in New York City. He was a member of the President's Foreign Intelligence Advisory Board in 1973–76, and served as chairman in 1976–77. He is married, has one daughter, and resides in New York City.

HOWARD H. BAKER, JR. is a senior partner in the law firm Vinson & Elkins in Washington, D.C. He served as a United States senator from Tennessee from 1966 to 1985. He was minority leader in 1977–81 and majority leader in 1981–85. He is married, has two children, and resides in Washington, D.C.

WILLIAM O. BAKER is a research chemist and was chairman of the board of Bell Telephone Laboratories. He was a member of the President's Foreign Intelligence Advisory Board in 1959–77. He is married, has one son, and resides in Morristown, New Jersey.

W. GLENN CAMPBELL has been director of the Hoover Institution on War, Revolution, and Peace at Stanford University since 1960, and has served as the chairman of the President's Intelligence Oversight Board since 1981. He was a member of the National Science Board, National Science Foundation, in 1972–78. He is married, has three children, and resides in Stanford, California.

JOHN S. FOSTER, JR. is vice-president, Science and Technology, TRW, Inc. He was director of Defense Research and Engineering for the Department of Defense in 1965–73. Mr. Foster served as a member of the President's Foreign Intelligence Advisory Board in 1973–77. He is married, has five children, and resides in Cleveland, Ohio.

HENRY A. KISSINGER is chairman of Kissinger and Associates, Inc. He was secretary of state in 1973–77 and served as the assistant to the President for National Security Affairs from 1969–74. He is married, has two children, and resides in New York City.

CLARE BOOTHE LUCE was a member of the President's Foreign Intelligence Advisory Board in 1973–77. She is a playwright and journalist. She was also a member of Congress in 1943–47 and ambassador to Italy in 1953–57. She resides in Washington, D.C.

WILLIAM FRENCH SMITH is a partner in the firm of Gibson, Dunn, and Crutcher of Los Angeles. Previously he served as attorney general of the United States in 1981–85. He is married, has four children, and resides in San Marino, California.

ALBERT D. WHEELON is senior vice-president and group president of the Space and Communications Group of Hughes Aircraft Company. He was deputy director for science and technology at the Central Intelligence Agency in 1962–64. He is married, has two children, and resides in Los Angeles, California.

JEANE J. KIRKPATRICK was the representative of the United States to the United Nations and a member of the cabinet (1981–85). She has resumed her position as Leavey Professor at Georgetown University and as senior fellow at the American Enterprise Institute. She is married, has three children, and resides in Bethesda, Maryland.

BERNARD A. SCHRIEVER was commander of the U.S. Air Force Systems Command in 1961–66. He retired from the air force with the rank of general. He was chairman of the President's Advisory Council on Management Improvement and is currently serving as a member of the National Commission on Space. He is married, has three children, and resides in Washington, D.C.

JAMES Q. WILSON is Henry Lee Shattuck Professor of Government at Harvard University and James Collins Professor of Management at UCLA. He is chairman of the Board of Directors of the Police Foundation and former chairman of the White House Task Force on Crime and National Advisory Council on Drug Abuse Prevention. He is married, has two children, and resides in Belmont, Massachusetts.

ALBERT J. WOHLSTETTER is director of research at PAN Heuristics, Marina del Rey, California. He held the University Professorship for 15 years at the University of Chicago, and before that was a member of the Research Council and assistant to the president at Rand Corporation. He is married, has one child, and resides in Los Angeles, California.

Glossary

Accommodation address. A mail address, usually a post office box, for communication between agents.

AFSA. Armed Forces Security Agency. The predecessor of the National Security Agency (NSA); it was created in 1949 to consolidate the cryptologic effort.

Agent. An individual who acts under the direction of an intelligence agency or security service to obtain, or assist in obtaining, information for intelligence or counterintelligence purposes.

Agent of influence. An individual who can be used to covertly influence foreign officials, opinion molders, organizations, or pressure groups in a way that generally will advance U.S. government objectives, or to undertake specific action in support of U.S. government objectives.

Analysis. A stage in the intelligence processing cycle whereby collected information is reviewed to identify significant facts. The information is compared and collated with other data, and conclusions that also incorporate the memory and judgment of the intelligence analyst are derived from it.

ASA. Army Security Agency. One of the Service Cryptologic Agencies; its collection activities are under the authority of the Director of NSA in his dual role as Chief of the Central Security Service (CSS).

Assessment. Part of the intelligence process whereby an analyst determines the reliability or validity of a piece of information; also, a statement resulting from this process.

Asset. Any resource—a person, group, relationship, instrument, installation, or supply—at the disposition of an intelligence agency for use in an operational or support role. The term is normally applied to a person who is contributing to a CIA clandestine mission, but is not a fully controlled agent of CIA.

Bigot list. A restrictive list of persons who have access to a particular and highly sensitive class of information. *Bigot* is read to mean *narrow*.

Black. Indicates reliance on illegal concealment of an activity, rather than on cover.

Black bag job. Warrantless surreptitious entry, especially conducted for purposes other than microphone installation, such as physical search and seizure or photographing documents.

Black propaganda. Propaganda that purports to emanate from a source other than the true one. If no attribution is given, it is called *gray propaganda*.

Blow. To expose—often unintentionally—personnel, installations, or other elements of a clandestine activity or organization.

Bug. A concealed listening device or microphone or other audio surveillance device; also, to install the means for audio surveillance of a subject or target.

Bugged. Contains a concealed listening device.

Burst transmission. A preset message transmitted rapidly to thwart hostile direction-finding surveillance.

Case. An intelligence operation in its entirety; also, a record of the development, methods, and objectives of an operation.

Case officer. A staff employee of the CIA responsible for handling agents.

CIG. Central Intelligence Group. The immediate predecessor of CIA. President Truman established it by executive order on January 22, 1946. It operated under the National Intelligence Authority (NIA), which was created at the same time. *See also* NIA.

Cipher. Any cryptographic system in which arbitrary symbols or groups of symbols represent units of plain text.

Clandestine intelligence. Intelligence information collected via covert resources.

Classification. The determination that official information requires, in the interest of national security, a specific degree of protection from unauthorized disclosure, coupled with a designation signifying that such a determination has been made. The designation normally is termed a *security classification*.

Code. A system of communication in which arbitrary groups of symbols represent units of plain text. Codes may be used for brevity or security.

Code word. A word assigned a classification and a classified meaning to safeguard intentions and information regarding a planned operation.

Collection. The acquisition of information by any means and its delivery to the proper intelligence processing unit for use in the production of intelligence.

COMINT. Communications intelligence. Technical and intelligence information derived from foreign communications by someone other than the intended recipient; sometimes used interchangeably with SIGINT. It does not include foreign press, propaganda, or public broadcasts.

Company, the. Insiders' name for the Central Intelligence Agency.

Compartmentation. The practice of establishing channels for handling sensitive intelligence information. The channels are limited to individuals with a specific need for such information and who are therefore given special security clearances in order to have access to it.

COMSEC. Communications security. The protection of U.S. telecommunications from exploitation by foreign intelligence services and from unauthorized disclosure. COMSEC is one of the mission responsibilities of NSA. It includes cryptosecurity, transmission security, emission security, and physical security of classified equipment, material, and documents.

Consumer. A person or agency that uses information or intelligence produced either by its own staff or other agencies.

Control. Physical or psychological pressure exerted on an agent or group to ensure that the agent or group responds to the direction from an intelligence agency or service.

Co-opted worker. A citizen of a country who is not an officer or employee of the country's intelligence service, but who assists that service on a temporary or regular basis. In most circumstances, a co-opted worker is an official of the country, but might also be a tourist or student, for example.

Counterespionage. Those aspects of counterintelligence concerned with aggressive operations against another intelligence service to reduce its effectiveness or to detect and neutralize foreign espionage. This is done by identification, penetration, manipulation, deception, and repression of individuals, groups, or organizations conducting or suspected of conducting espionage activities in order to destroy, neutralize, exploit, or prevent such espionage activities.

Counterinsurgency. Military, paramilitary, political, economic, psychological, civic, and any other actions taken by a government to defeat rebellion and subversion within a country.

Counterintelligence. Activities conducted to destroy the effectiveness of foreign intelligence operations and to protect information against espionage, individuals against subversion, and installations against sabotage; also refers to information developed by or used in counterintelligence operations. *See also* Counterespionage.

Courier. A messenger responsible for the secure physical transmission and delivery of documents and material.

Cousins. British Secret Intelligence Service (SIS) name for CIA.

Cover. A protective guise used by a person, organization, or installation to prevent identification with clandestine activities and to conceal the true affiliation of personnel and the true sponsorship of their activities.

Covert action. Any clandestine activity designed to influence foreign governments, events, organizations, or persons in support of U.S. foreign policy, and that conceals the identity of the sponsor or else permits the sponsor's plausible denial of the operation; sometimes called *covert operations, clandestine operations,* and *clandestine activity.*

Cryptanalysis. The breaking of codes and ciphers into plain text without initial knowledge of the key employed in the encryption.

CRYPTO. A designation applied to classified, cryptographic information that involves special rules for access and handling.

Cryptography. The enciphering of a plain text so that it will be unintelligible to an unauthorized reader or recipient.

Cut-out. A person used to conceal contact between members of a clandestine activity or organization.

Damage assessment. An evaluation of the impact of a compromise in terms of loss of intelligence information, sources, or methods, which may describe and/or recommend measures to minimize damage and prevent future compromises.

Dangle. Someone who intentionally draws the attention of a hostile intelligence service so that, through mere contact, information may be learned about that service.

DCI. Director of Central Intelligence. The President's principal foreign intelligence advisor, appointed by him with the consent of the Senate to be the head of the intelligence community and Director of the Central Intelligence Agency and to discharge those authorities and responsibilities as they are prescribed by law and by Presidential and National Security Council directives.

DCID. Director of Central Intelligence Directive. A directive issued by the DCI that outlines general policies and procedures to be followed by intelligence agencies under his direction; usually more specific than a National Security Council Intelligence Directive (*see* NSCID).

Defector. A person who, for political or other reasons, repudiates and flees his country, usually to an adversary nation interested in what intelligence he could provide about the country of origin.

Defense intelligence community. Refers to the Defense Intelligence Agency (DIA), the National Security Agency (NSA), and the military services' intelligence offices including Department of Defense (DOD) collectors of specialized intelligence through reconnaissance programs.

DIA. Defense Intelligence Agency. Department of Defense agency responsible for producing military intelligence, created by directive of the Secretary of Defense in 1961.

Double agent. A person engaging in clandestine activity for two or more intelligence or security services who provide information to one service about the other, or about each service to the other, and who is wittingly or unwittingly manipulated by one service against the other.

Drop. Clandestine transference of intelligence information. Leaving material in a secret place for pick-up later is a *dead drop,* as opposed to a *live drop,* when people meet to pass material.

ECM. Electronic countermeasures. That division of electronic warfare involving actions taken to prevent or reduce an adversary's effective use of the electromagnetic spectrum. Electronic countermeasures include electronic jamming, which is the deliberate radiation, reradiation, or reflection of electromagnetic energy with the object of impairing the uses of electronic equipment used by an adversary; and electronic deception, which is similar but is intended to mislead an adversary in the interpretation of information received by his electronic system.

Elicitation. The acquisition of intelligence from a person or group which does not disclose the intent of the interview or conversation; a human intelligence (*see* HUMINT) collection technique generally of an overt nature, unless the collector is other than what he or she purports to be.

ELINT. Electronic intelligence. Technical and intelligence information derived from the collection (or interception) and processing of foreign electromagnetic radiations (noncommunications) emanating from sources such as radar.

Espionage. Clandestine collection of intelligence.

Executive action. Generally a euphemism for *assassination,* used by the CIA to describe a program aimed at overthrowing certain foreign leaders, by assassinating them if necessary.

Fabricator. An agent who provides false information.

False flag. A recruitment involving a deliberate misrepresentation of one's actual employer to achieve the recruitment.

Farm, the. Training school for CIA in Virginia.

Flap. A commotion, controversy, or publicity that is the result of a bungled intelligence operation.

Flaps and seals man. Expert at undetected opening and closing of the mails.

Flutter. To conduct a polygraph or lie detector test.

Gray propaganda. See Black propaganda.

Honey trap. Operation to compromise an opponent sexually.

HUMINT. Human intelligence. Intelligence information derived from human sources.

IC. Intelligence community. Refers, in the aggregate, to the following executive branch organizations: the Central Intelligence Agency, the National Security Agency, the Defense Intelligence Agency, offices within the Department of Defense for the collection of specialized national foreign intelligence through reconnaissance programs, the Bureau of Intelligence and Research of the Department of State, intelligence elements of the military services, intelligence elements of the Federal Bureau of Investigation, intelligence elements of the Department of the Treasury, intelligence elements of the Department of Energy, intelligence elements of the Drug Enforcement Administration, and staff elements of the Office of the Director of Central Intelligence.

Illegal. An officer or employee of an intelligence organization who is dispatched abroad and who has no overt connection with the intelligence organization with which he is connected or with the government operating that intelligence organization.

Illegal residency. An intelligence apparatus established in a foreign country and composed of one or more intelligence officers, and which has no apparent connection with the sponsoring intelligence organization or with the government of the country operating the intelligence organization.

Infiltration. The placing of an agent or other person in a target area within hostile territory or within targeted groups or organizations.

Informant. A person who wittingly or unwittingly provides information to an agent, a clandestine service, or police. In reporting such information, this person will often be cited as the source.

Informer. One who intentionally discloses information about other persons or activities to police or a security service (such as the FBI), usually for a financial reward.

INR. Bureau of Intelligence and Research. The U.S. Department of State's intelligence service.

Intelligence cycle. The steps by which information is assembled, converted into intelligence, and made available to consumers. The cycle comprises four basic phases: (1) *direction,* the determination of intelligence requirements, preparation of a collection plan, tasking of collection agencies, and a continuous check on the productivity of these agencies; (2) *collection,* the exploitation of information sources and the delivery of the collected information to the proper intelligence processing unit for use in the production of intelligence; (3) *processing,* the steps whereby information becomes intelligence through evaluation, analysis, integration, and interpretation; and (4) *dissemination,* the distribution of information or intelligence products in oral, written, or graphic form to departmental and agency intelligence consumers. *See also* Consumer.

Intelligence estimate. An appraisal of intelligence elements relating to a specific situation or condition to determine the courses of action open to an enemy or potential enemy and the probable order of their adoption.

Intelligence officer. A professional employee of an intelligence organization who engages in intelligence activities.

Interception. Generally refers to the collection of electromagnetic signals such as radio communications by sophisticated collection equipment without the knowledge of the communicants for the production of certain forms of signals intelligence.

Interrogation. A systematic effort to procure information by direct questioning of a person under the control of the questioner.

Legend. Invented name and biography to hide the identity of a spy.

MI. Military intelligence. Basic, current, or estimative intelligence on any foreign military or military-related situation or activity.

Mole. Hostile spy who burrows into an intelligence organization to report to an enemy one.

Monitoring. The observing of, listening to, or recording of foreign or domestic communications for intelligence collection or intelligence security (e.g., COMSEC) purposes.

Music box. Radio transmitter.

National intelligence. Intelligence produced by the CIA that bears on the broad aspects of U.S. national policy and national security. It is of concern to more than one department or agency.

NFIB. National Foreign Intelligence Board. A body formed to provide the Director of Central Intelligence with advice concerning: production, review, and coordination of national foreign intelligence; the National Foreign Intelligence Program budget; interagency exchanges of foreign intelligence information; arrangements with foreign governments on intelligence matters; the protection of intelligence sources or methods; activities of common concern; and such other matters as are referred to it by the DCI. The board is composed of the DCI (chairman) and other appropriate officers of the Central Intelligence Agency, the Office of the DCI, Department of State, Department of Defense, Department of Justice, Department of the Treasury, Department of Energy, the offices within the Department of Defense for reconnaissance programs, the Defense Intelligence Agency, the National Security Agency, and the Federal Bureau of Investigation; senior intelligence officers of the army, navy, and air force participate as observers; a representative of the Assistant to the President for National Security Affairs may also attend meetings as an observer.

NIA. National Intelligence Authority. An executive council created by President Truman's executive order of January 22, 1946, which had authority over the simultaneously created Central Intelligence Group (see CIG); predecessor of the National Security Council.

NIE. National Intelligence Estimate. An estimate authorized by the DCI of the capabilities, vulnerabilities, and probable courses of action of foreign nations; represents the composite view of the intelligence community.

NSA. National Security Agency. The most secret U.S. intelligence agency, it is responsible for all U.S. communications security activities, including developing codes and ciphers, and for developing foreign intelligence information; established October 24, 1952, by President Truman to replace the Armed Forces Security Agency (see AFSA).

NSC. National Security Council. Established by the National Security Act of 1947 and placed within the Executive Office of the President in 1949, NSC advises the President on matters relating to national security with respect to the integration of domestic, foreign, and military policies; comprised of the President, Vice-President, Secretary of State, and Secretary of Defense, with the Director of Central Intelligence and Chairman of the Joint Chiefs of Staff acting as advisors.

NSCID. National Security Council Intelligence Directive. Intelligence guidelines issued by the NSC to intelligence agencies. NSCIDs are often augmented by more specific Director of Central Intelligence Directives and by internal departmental or agency regulations. See also DCID.

Order of battle. Information regarding the identity, strength, command structure, and disposition of personnel, units, and equipment of any military force.

OSS. Office of Strategic Services. The U.S. intelligence service active during World War II; established by President Roosevelt in June 1942 and disbanded by President Truman on October 1, 1945.

Paper mill. A fabricator who provides false information consistently and in volume; see also Fabricator.

Paroles. Key words for mutual identification among agents.

Penetration. The recruitment of agents within or the planting of agents or technical monitoring devices within a target organization to gain access to its secrets or to influence its activities.

PHOTINT. Photographic intelligence. Information or intelligence derived from photography through photographic interpretation.

Pickle Factory. Insiders' name for the Central Intelligence Agency.

Pitch. The act of persuading a person to be an agent; a pitch made without the benefit of any prior cultivation of the person in question is a *cold pitch.*

Plain text. Unencrypted communications; specifically, the original message of a cryptogram expressed in ordinary language.

Plumbing. Assets or services supporting the clandestine operations of CIA field stations, such as safe houses, unaccountable funds, investigative persons, surveillance teams.

Pocket litter. The misleading documents and materials an agent carries to protect his identity and background if apprehended.

Principal agent. An agent who recruits other agents and then manages the resulting network.

Product. Finished intelligence reports disseminated by intelligence agencies to appropriate consumers.

Proprietaries. Ostensibly private commercial entities capable of doing business, which are established and controlled by intelligence services to conceal governmental affiliation of intelligence personnel and/or governmental sponsorship of certain activities in support of clandestine operations.

Raven. Male seducer to lure a woman into a honey trap; see also Honey trap.

Raw intelligence. A colloquial term meaning collected intelligence information that has not yet been converted into intelligence.

Requirement. A general or specific request for intelligence information made by a member of the intelligence community.

Safe house. A seemingly innocent house or premises established by an intelligence organization for conducting clandestine or covert activity in relative security.

Sanitize. To delete from or revise a report or document to prevent identification of the intelligence sources and methods that contributed to or are dealt with in the report.

Secret writing. Messages written with an invisible substance, ranging from lemon juice to sophisticated chemicals that appear under certain conditions.

Sensitive. Requires special protection from disclosure, which could cause embarrassment, compromise, or threat to the security of the sponsoring power.

Sheep dipping. Using a military instrument (e.g., an airplane) or officer in clandestine operations, usually in a civilian capacity or under civilian cover, although the instrument or officer will covertly retain its or his military ownership or standing; also, placing individuals in organizations or groups in which they can become active in order to establish credentials so that they can be used to collect information of intelligence interest on similar groups.

Shoe. False passport.

SIGINT. Signals intelligence. The interception, processing, analysis, and dissemination of information derived from foreign electrical communications and other signals; includes communications intelligence (see COMINT) and electronics intelligence (see ELINT).

Sleeper. A previously placed spy ready to be activated at a suitable moment.

Source. A person, device, system, or activity from which intelligence information is obtained.

Spook. American slang for a spy.

Sterilize. To remove from material to be used in overt and clandestine actions any marks or devices that can identify it as originating with the sponsoring organization or nation.

Strategic intelligence. Intelligence required for the formation of policy and military plans and operations at the national and international levels.

Stringer. An occasional or free-lance spy.

Surveillance. Systematic monitoring or observation of a target.

Swallow. Female seducer to lure a man into a honey trap; *see also* Honey trap.

Tactical intelligence. Intelligence supporting military plans and operations at the military unit level. Tactical intelligence and strategic intelligence differ only in scope, point of view, and level of employment.

Target. A person, agency, facility, area, or country against which intelligence operations are directed.

Targeting. With regard to COMINT, the intentional selection and/or collection of telecommunications for intelligence purposes.

Target of opportunity. An entity (e.g., governmental entity, installation, political organization, or individual) that becomes available to an intelligence agency or service by chance, and provides the opportunity for the collection of needed information.

Tradecraft. The techniques of espionage; also, the technical equipment used in such activity, such as electronic eavesdropping equipment and miniaturized radios.

Turned. Persuaded or bribed to change sides.

Walk-in. Anyone who walks in volunteering services or information, usually a foreigner who enters another nation's embassy.

Watchers. Officers keeping persons under surveillance.

Watch list. A list of words, such as names, entities, or phrases, that can be employed by a computer to select required information from a mass of data.

Acronyms

AFSA	Armed Forces Security Agency
ASA	Army Security Agency
CIA	Central Intelligence Agency
CIG	Central Intelligence Group
COI	Office of the Coordinator of Information (predecessor of OSS)
COMINT	Communications intelligence
COMSEC	Communications security
DCI	Director of Central Intelligence
DCID	Director of Central Intelligence Directive
DDA	CIA Directorate of Administration; also, the Deputy Director of DDA
DDCI	Deputy Director of Central Intelligence
DDI	CIA Directorate of Intelligence; also, the Deputy Director of DDI
DDO	CIA Directorate of Operations; also, the Deputy Director of DDO
DDS&T	CIA Directorate of Science and Technology; also, the Deputy Director of DDS&T
DEA	Drug Enforcement Administration
DIA	Defense Intelligence Agency
DOD	Department of Defense
ECM	Electronic countermeasures
ELINT	Electronic intelligence
FBI	Federal Bureau of Investigation
GRU	Main Intelligence Directorate of the Red Army; in Russian, *Glavnoye Razvedyvatelnoye Upravleniye*
HUMINT	Human intelligence
IC	Intelligence community
INR	Bureau of Intelligence and Research (of the Department of State)
IOB	Intelligence Oversight Board
KGB	Soviet Committee for State Security; in Russian, *Komitet Gosudarstvennoy Bezopasnosti*
MI	Military intelligence
NATO	North Atlantic Treaty Organization
NFIB	National Foreign Intelligence Board
NIA	National Intelligence Authority
NIE	National Intelligence Estimate
NKVD	People's Commissariat for Internal Affairs (KGB precursor); in Russian, *Narodny Kommissariat Vnutrennykh Del*
NSA	National Security Agency
NSC	National Security Council
NSCID	National Security Council Intelligence Directive
OSS	Office of Strategic Services
PFIAB	President's Foreign Intelligence Advisory Board
PHOTINT	Photographic intelligence
SI	Secret Intelligence (unit of OSS)
SIGINT	Signals intelligence
X-2	Counterintelligence (unit of OSS)

255